TRANSGENDER HISTORY

Transgender History
© 2008 Susan Stryker

Published by Seal Press
a member of the Perseus Books Group
1700 Fourth Street
Berkeley, CA 94710

10 9 8 7 6 5 4 3 2

Library of Congress Cataloging-in-Publication Data

Stryker, Susan.
Transgender history / by Susan Stryker.
    p. cm.
ISBN-13: 978-1-58005-224-5
ISBN-10: 1-58005-224-X
1. Transgenderism—History. 2. Gender identity—History. 3. Transgender people—
History. I. Title.
HQ77.9.S77 2008
306.76'8—dc22
                    2008005316

Cover design by Kate Basart, Union Pageworks
Cover illustration © Lauren Simkin Berke c/o rileyillustration.com
Book design by Mike Walters
Printed in the United States of America
Distributed by Publishers Group West

TRANSGENDER HISTORY

SUSAN STRYKER

SEAL
Studies

This book is dedicated to all the trans people who lived the lives that made the history I've outlined here, and to the community activists, too numerous to mention, who continue to advance the cause of social justice for transgender people everywhere.

CONTENTS

PROLOGUE

THE BRIEF HISTORY OF THE TRANSGENDER MOVEMENT in the United States presented in this book has a lot of personal significance for me. Piecing the story together has been the main focus of my professional life as a historian for nearly twenty years. But as a transsexual woman, I've also been a participant in making that history, along with thousands of other people. What I have to say is colored by my own involvement in that movement, by my life experiences, and by the particular ways that I consider myself to be transgendered.

I'm one of those people who, from earliest memory, always felt I was a girl even though I had a male body at birth and everybody considered me to be a boy. I didn't have an explanation for those feelings when I was younger, and after a lifetime of reflection and study I'm still open-minded now about how best to explain them. I hid those feelings from absolutely everybody until I was in my late teens, and I didn't start coming out publicly as transgendered until the late 1980s, when I was almost thirty. I'd never knowingly met another transgender person before that time.

I started living 24/7 as an openly transsexual lesbian woman in San Francisco in 1991–92, just as I was finishing up my PhD in United States history at the University of California—Berkeley. At the time, it wasn't a great career move, just something I needed to do for my own personal sense of well-being. As wonderful as it was for me to finally feel right about how I presented myself to others and how others perceived me, making the transition from living as a man to living as a woman had some huge negative effects on my life. Like many transgender people, I spent years being marginally employed because of other people's discomfort, ignorance, and prejudice. Transitioning made relationships with many friends and relatives more difficult. It made me more vulnerable to certain kinds of legal discrimination, and it sometimes made me feel unsafe in public.

Because I lived in the world as a well-educated white man before coming out as the woman I always felt myself to be, I have a very clear measuring stick for gauging sexism and misogyny. My transgender experience is a part of the strong commitment I feel to feminist activism that aims to make the world a better place for all women and girls. Because I now live in the world as a woman who loves women, and because there are times (more common in the past than now) when I've been perceived as an effeminate gay man, I also have a direct experience of homophobia. My transgender experience is thus also part of why I feel a strong commitment to lesbian and gay rights. Although I can't claim that being transgendered gives me any special insight into other kinds of discrimination (based on race or national origin, for example), I have experienced the injustice of being the target of irrational hatred, and this has sensitized me to situations where I see other people being treated unjustly. My transgender experience makes me want to be a good ally to other people who experience forms of discrimination different from my own. It makes me want to help build a world that honors many kinds of human differences. My own vision of a transgender social justice movement is one that addresses the specific kinds of problems transgender people can face in the world, by seeing them as structurally related to problems of racism, poverty, and other systemic injustices.

Starting in the early 1990s, I've had the privilege of using my education as part of a transgender movement for social change. I became a community-based historian, theorist, media-maker, and activist who chronicles transgender experience. I've lived for many years in a very stimulating genderqueer community in San Francisco, which has been exciting intellectually and artistically as well as politically and socially. A lot of my ideas and opinions about gender and politics crystallized there during the first half of the 1990s, so what I have to say is both generationally and geographically specific—though I do try to stay current in my thinking by continually revising what I learned from my own formative experiences in light of more recent trends, ideas, and developments. I travel a lot and talk to a lot of different kinds of transgender people around the world, and I spend way too much time prowling around the Internet.

By the later 1990s, more and more people were beginning to see transgender issues as a cutting-edge topic, and I was fortunate to receive funding from the Ford Foundation/Social Science Research Council to conduct research on transgender history in San Francisco— research that informs what I have to say in this book. Between 1999 and 2003, I worked as executive director of the GLBT Historical Society in San Francisco, which has one of the world's best collections of transgender, lesbian, gay, and bisexual historical materials; there I had further opportunities to do ongoing archival research and to talk with other scholars and activists in the rapidly expanding field of transgender studies. A few years later, in 2005, a friend and I made a public television documentary about the 1966 Compton's Cafeteria riot, then a little-known event in transgender history, which I had uncovered during my years of research. Through the years, I also wrote a few books and articles and edited a couple of anthologies and special journal issues on various transgender and queer topics. Now, as the first decade of the twenty-first century is speeding toward its close, I find myself, at least for now, teaching transgender theory and history as a professor of gender and women's studies. Writing this book is a way for me to summarize some of what I've gleaned from the life I've lived during the past twenty years and to pass it along to others who might find it useful or interesting.

CHAPTER 1

AN INTRODUCTION TO TRANSGENDER TERMS AND CONCEPTS

Foundations of a Movement

Because "transgender" is a word that has come into widespread use only in the past couple of decades, its meanings are still under construction. I use it in this book to refer to people who move away from the gender they were assigned at birth, people who cross over (*trans-*) the boundaries constructed by their culture to define and contain that gender. Some people move away from their birth-assigned gender because they feel strongly that they properly belong to another gender in which it would be better for them to live; others want to strike out toward some new location, some space not yet clearly defined or concretely occupied; still others simply feel the need to get away from the conventional expectations bound up with the gender that was initially put upon them. In any case, it is *the movement across a socially imposed boundary away from an unchosen starting place*—rather than any particular destination or mode of transition—that best characterizes the concept of "transgender" that I want to develop here.

Most often, transgender-related topics have been written about as personal issues—something that an individual experiences inwardly and works to bring into social reality by sharing it with others. There are many autobiographies of people who have "changed sex" and an increasing number of self-help guidebooks for people contemplating such a change. There are now a lot of good documentary films and television shows about transgender people—as well as a lot of exploitative or sensationalistic mass media representations—the vast majority of which focus on the triumphs and tribulations of particular individuals. There is also an extensive medical and psychological literature that treats transgender phenomena as a personal (and pathological) deviation from social norms of healthy gender expression. This book takes a different approach to transgender topics from all those mentioned above. It focuses instead on the collective political history of transgender social change activism in the United States—that is, on efforts to make it easier and safer and more acceptable for the people who need to cross gender boundaries to be able to do so. It's not designed, however, to be a comprehensive account of transgender history. The goals are to provide a basic chronology from the nineteenth century to the twenty-first, and to focus on a number of key events or personalities that help link transgender history to the history of minority movements for social change, to the history of sexuality and gender, and to feminist thought and politics.

Back in the 1970s, the feminist movement tossed around the slogan "The personal is political." Most feminists back then were critical of transgender practices such as cross-dressing, taking hormones to change the gendered appearance of the body, having genital or chest surgery, or living as a member of a gender other than one's birth-assigned gender. They considered such practices to be "personal solutions" to the inner experience of distress about experiencing gender-based oppression—that is, they thought that a female-bodied person passing as a man was just trying to escape the poor pay (or no pay) of "women's work" or to move about more safely in a world that was hostile to women; a feminine male-bodied person, they thought, should work for the social acceptability of sissies and be proudly effeminate instead of pretending to be a "normal" woman, or a "real" one. Feminism, on the other hand, aimed to systematically dismantle the social structures that created gender-based oppression in the first place and that made women the "second sex." Mainstream feminism wanted to raise women's consciousnesses about their own private suffering by grounding that experience in a political analysis of the categorical oppression of all women. It wanted to offer men an education in feminist values in order to eradicate the sexism and misogyny they (knowingly or unknowingly) directed at women. Feminism was, and still is, a movement to change the world for the better.

One of the goals of this book is to situate transgender social change activism within an expanded feminist framework. Doing so requires us to think in different ways about *how* the personal is political, and about what constitutes gender-based oppression. Transgender feminism, though it has its roots in the feminist radicalism of the late 1960s, is part of what is sometimes now known as the third wave of feminism (the first wave of feminism focused on dress reform, access to education, political equality, and, above all, suffrage in the nineteenth and early twentieth centuries; the second wave, also known as the women's movement of the 1960s and '70s, addressed a wide range of issues, including equal pay, sexual and reproductive freedom, recognition of women's unpaid work in the household, better media representations of women, and rape and domestic violence). Third wave feminism has been, in part, a generational response to some of the perceived shortcomings of the second wave, particularly the tendency of second wave feminists to overlook differences among women in their eagerness to see "woman" as a unifying political category. Third wave feminism has been more attuned to the intersections of race, class, and sexuality within gender and more receptive to critical and theoretical work in gender studies that calls into question the usefulness of "woman" as the foundation of all feminist politics. Contemporary transgender movements for social change draw on many of the insights and critiques of third wave feminism.

A feminism that makes room for transgender people still fights to dismantle the structures that prop up gender as a system of oppression, but it does so without passing moral judgment on people who feel the need to change their birth-assigned gender. To reevaluate the relationship between transgender and feminist politics, it is essential to acknowledge that how each of us experiences and understands our gender identity—our sense of being a man or a woman or something that resists those terms—really is a very idiosyncratic personal matter. It

A Biological Basis?

Many people believe that gender identity—the subjective sense of being a man or a woman or both or neither—is rooted in biology, although what the biological "cause" of gender identity might be has never been proven. Many other people understand gender to be more like language than like biology; that is, while they understand us humans to have a biological capacity to use language, they point out we are not born with a hard-wired language "preinstalled" in our brains. Likewise, while we have a biological capacity to identify with and to learn to "speak" from a particular location in a cultural gender system, we don't come into the world with a predetermined gender identity.

Evolutionary biologist Joan Roughgarden suggests a way to blend learned versus innate models of gender identity development. In *Evolution's Rainbow: Diversity, Gender, and Sexuality in Nature and People*, she writes:

> When does gender identity form during development? Gender identity, like other aspects of temperament, presumably awaits the third trimester, when the brain as a whole is growing. . . . The time around birth may be when the brain's gender identity is being organized. . . . I envision gender identity as a cognitive lens. When a baby opens his or her eyes after birth and looks around, whom will the baby emulate and whom will he or she merely notice? Perhaps a male baby will emulate his father or

is something prior to, or underlying, our political actions in the world and not in itself a reflection of our political beliefs. Nontransgender people, after all, think of themselves as having a gender, or being a gender, and nobody asks them to defend the political correctness of their "choice" in the matter or thinks that their having a sense of being gendered somehow compromises or invalidates their other values and commitments. Being transgendered is like being gay—some people are just "that way," though most people aren't. We can be curious about *why* some people are gay or transgendered, and we can propose all kinds of theories or tell lots of interesting stories about how it's possible *other men, perhaps not, and a female baby her mother or other women, perhaps not. I imagine that a lens in the brain controls who to focus on as a "tutor." Transgender identity is then the acceptance of a tutor from the opposite sex. Degrees of transgender identity, and of gender variance generally, reflect different degrees of single-mindedness in the selection of the tutor's gender. The development of gender identity thus depends on both brain state and early postnatal experience, because brain state indicates what the lens is, and environmental experience supplies the image to be photographed through that lens and ultimately developed immutably into brain circuitry. Once gender identity is set, like other basic aspects of temperament, life proceeds from there.*

Science writer Deborah Rudacille became convinced that environmental factors helped explain the seeming increase in the prevalence of reported transgender phenomena while researching her book *The Riddle of Gender: Science, Activism, and Transgender Rights*. Rudacille draws on the 2001 paper "Endocrine Disrupting Chemicals and Transsexualism," in which author Christine Johnson posits a causal link between the "reproductive, behavioral, and anatomical effects" of exposure to chemicals commonly found in pesticides and food additives and "the expression of gender identity and other disorders such as reproductive failure." Rudacille links transgenderism to falling sperm counts among human males, to rising numbers of alligators with micropenises; hermaphroditic birds, fish, and amphibians; and to other anomalies purportedly associated with endocrine-disrupting chemicals in the environment.

to be transgendered, but ultimately we simply need to accept that some minor fraction of the population (perhaps including ourselves) simply *is* "that way."

Because members of minority groups are, by definition, less common than members of their corresponding majority groups, members of minorities often experience discrimination and prejudice. Society tends to be organized in ways that (either deliberately or unintentionally) favor the majority; ignorance or misinformation about a less common way of being in the world can perpetuate harmful stereotypes and mischaracterizations. People who feel the need to resist their birth-assigned gender or to live as a member of another gender have tended to encounter significant forms of discrimination and prejudice—even religious condemnation. Because most people have great difficulty recognizing the humanity of another person if they cannot recognize that person's gender, the gender-changing person can evoke in others a primordial fear of monstrosity, or loss of humanness. That gut-level fear can manifest itself as hatred, outrage, panic, or disgust, which may then translate into physical or emotional violence directed against the person who is perceived as not-quite-human. Such people are often shunned and may be denied such basic needs as housing or employment. Within modern bureaucratic society, many kinds of routine administrative procedures make life very difficult for people who cross the social boundaries of their birth-assigned genders. Birth certificates, school and medical records, professional credentials, passports, driver's licenses, and other such documents provide a composite portrait of each of us as a person with a particular gender, and when these records have noticeable discrepancies or omissions, all kinds of problems can result—inability to marry, for example, or to cross national borders, or qualify for jobs, or gain access to needed social services, or secure legal custody of one's children. Because transgender people typically lack the same kind of support that fully accepted members of society automatically expect, they may be more likely to engage in risky or harmful behaviors and consequently may wind up having more health problems or trouble with the law—which only compounds their already considerable difficulties.

In the United States, members of minority groups often try to oppose or change discriminatory practices and prejudicial attitudes by banding together to offer one another mutual support, to voice their issues in public, to raise money to improve their collective lot in life, to form organizations that address their specific unmet needs, or to participate in electoral politics or lobby for the passage of protective legislation. Some engage in more radical or militant kinds of activism. Some members of the minority group make art or write literature that changes the way others think of them and the issues they face.

Some do the intellectual and theoretical work of analyzing the roots of their particular forms of social oppression and devising strategies and policies that will bring about a better future. Others direct their attention toward promoting self-acceptance and a sense of self-worth among members of the minority community who have internalized disempowering attitudes or beliefs about their difference from the dominant majority. In short, a multidimensional activist movement for social change often begins to take shape. Just such a movement to address transgender-related social justice issues developed in the United States in the decades after World War II.

Terms and Definitions

Before moving on to a discussion of that history, however, it would be worthwhile to spend a little time defining some of the common terms, concepts, and assumptions that I will be using throughout this book. Because transgender issues touch on fundamental questions of human existence, they take us into areas that we rarely consider carefully; usually, we simply experience these things without thinking about them too much—as we do with gravity, for example, or breathing. In the everyday course of events, most people have no reason to ask questions such as "What makes a man a man, or a woman a woman?" or "How is my body related to my social role?" or even "How do I know what my gender is?" Rather, we just go about our everyday business without cause to question the unexamined assumptions that form part of our working reality. But gender, like gravity or breathing, is a really complicated topic when you start taking it apart and breaking it down—as the following terms and definitions attest. In offering these handy thumbnail sketches of how I use certain key concepts, I nevertheless hope to complicate how we understand them and to begin introducing some of the arguments that will play themselves out in the chapters ahead.

Sex: Sex is not the same as gender, although many people use the terms interchangeably in everyday speech. Sex is generally considered biological, and gender is generally considered cultural (although that understanding is changing too). The words "male" and "female" refer to sex. Sex refers to reproductive capacity or potential—whether an individual body produces one or the other of the two specialized cells (egg or sperm) necessary for our species to physically reproduce itself. Sperm producers are said to be of the male sex, and egg producers are said to be of the female sex. This should not be taken to mean that there are only two kinds of bodies (male and female) or that all bodies are either one or the other of only two possible kinds of bodies. Bodies that mix physical characteristics of male or female, of which there are many different varieties, are said to be intersex (defined below). The sex status of any particular body is determined genetically, predominantly by the parts of the genes called the chromosomes (which have been given the identifying labels X and Y). The genetic or chromosomal sex of the body cannot (or at least cannot yet) be changed. In the contemporary United States, it is still widely believed that gender (defined below) is also determined by physical sex—meaning that a person with a male body is automatically considered a man and a person with a female body is automatically considered a woman—hence the common tendency to use the words "sex" and "gender" interchangeably. Some transgender people share this belief and assume that their need to cross gender boundaries has a physical, sex-linked cause. Other transgender people understand their sense of being transgendered to be entirely unrelated to biological sex differences and to be related instead to psychological and cultural processes. As mentioned above, it's possible to spin many different theories about why transgender people exist.

Intersex: Typically, being an egg-producing body or a sperm-producing body carries with it a number of related physical traits. Egg-producing bodies tend to have a uterus where the fused egg/sperm cells grow into new individuals, and they also tend to have milk-producing glands that provide nourishment for the young. Sperm-producing bodies tend to have a penis, which is useful for delivering the sperm to the uterus. These are, however, only the most common ways that natural selection has organized the reproductive anatomy of human bodies. When an egg and sperm cell come together, their chromosomes can combine in patterns (called "karyotypes") other than the two that result in typical male (XY) or typical female (XX) body types. Some genetic irregularities cause a body that is genetically XY (male) to look female at birth. Some bodies are born with genitals that look like a mixture of typically male and typically female shapes. Some genetically female bodies (XX) are born without vaginas, wombs, or ovaries. All of these variations on the most typical organization of human reproductive anatomy—along with many, many more—are called "intersex" conditions (and used to be called hermaphroditism). Some intersex people now prefer the medical term "DSD" (for Disorders of Sexual Development) to describe their sex status, but others reject this term as unduly pathologizing. Intersex conditions are far more common than most people realize; reliable estimates put the number at about one in two thousand births. Some transgender people who think their desire to cross gender boundaries has a biological cause consider themselves to have an intersex condition (current theories favor sex-linked neurological differences in the brain). Politically and sociologically, however, the transgender and intersex activist communities are quite different. Intersex activism, which will be discussed only tangentially in this book as it touches upon transgender issues, tends to focus on ending the practice of performing "normalization" surgery on infants born with noticeably ambiguous genitals; transgender people are rightly considered to face different kinds of problems with the medical establishment.

Morphology: Unlike genetic sex, a person's morphology, or the shape of the body that we typically associate with being male or female, can be modified in some respects—through surgery, hormones, exercise, clothing, and other methods. A typical adult male body shape is to have external genitalia (penis and testicles), a flat chest (no breasts), and a narrow pelvis. A typical female body shape is to have a vulva, a clitoris, breasts, and a broad pelvis. Morphology also refers to such aspects of body shape as the size of the hips relative to the waist, the breadth of the shoulders relative to height, the thickness of the limbs, and other gender-signifying features.

Secondary sex characteristics: Certain physical traits tend to be associated with genetic sex or reproductive potential, such as skin texture, body fat distribution, patterns of hair growth, or relative overall body size. Many of these physical traits are the effects of varying levels of hormones, the "chemical messengers" such as estrogen and testosterone that are produced by various endocrine glands throughout the body. Adjusting a person's hormone levels can change some (but not all) sex-linked traits. Secondary sex characteristics constitute perhaps the most socially significant part of morphology—taken together, they are the bodily "signs" that others read to guess at our sex, attribute gender to us, and assign us to the social category they understand to be most appropriate for us. Secondary sex characteristics are the aspect of our bodies that we all manipulate in an attempt to communicate to others our own sense of who we feel we are—whether we wear clothing with a neckline that emphasizes our cleavage, or whether we allow hair stubble to be visible on our faces. In this sense, all human bodies are modified bodies; all are shaped according to cultural practices. Shaping the body to represent oneself to others is such an important part of human culture that it's virtually impossible to practice any kind of body modification without other members of society having an opinion about whether the practice is good or bad, or right or wrong, depending on how or why one does it. Everything from cutting one's nails to cutting off one's leg falls somewhere on a spectrum

© powerHouse Books

Anonymous male cross-dresser at Casa Susanna, a private resort for cross-dressers in New York's Catskill Mountains from the late 1950s until the early 1960s.

of moral or ethical judgment. Consequently, many members of society have strong feelings and opinions about transgender body modification practices.

Gender: Gender is not the same as sex, though the two terms are often used interchangeably, even in technical or scholarly literature, creating a great deal of confusion. Gender is generally considered to be cultural, and sex, biological (though contemporary theories posit sex as a cultural category as well). The words "man" and "woman" refer to gender. No one is born a woman or a man—rather, as the saying goes, "one becomes one" through a complex process of socialization. Gender is the social organization of different kinds of bodies into different categories of people. (The English word "gender" is derived from *genre,* meaning "kind" or "type"). Historically and cross-culturally, there have been many different systems of organizing people into genders. Some cultures, including many Native American cultures, have had three or four social genders. Some attribute social gender to the work people do rather than to the bodies they live in. In some cultures people can change their social gender based on dreams or visions. In some they change it with a scalpel. The important things to bear in mind are that gender is historical (it changes through time), that it varies from place to place and culture to culture, and that it is contingent (it depends on a lot of different and seemingly unrelated things coming together). This takes us into one of the central issues of transgender politics—that the sex of the body does not bear any *necessary* or *deterministic* relationship to the social category in which that body lives. This assertion, drawn from the observation of human social variability, is political precisely because it contradicts the common belief that whether a person is a man or a woman in the social sense is fundamentally determined by the sex of the body. It's political in the additional sense that how a society organizes its members into categories based on their unchosen physical differences is never politically neutral. One of the main points of feminism is that societies tend to be organized in ways that are more exploitative of female bodies than of male bodies. Without disagreeing with that basic insight, a transgender perspective would also be sensitive to an additional dimension of gender oppression—that our culture today tries to reduce the wide range of livable body types into two and *only* two genders, one of which is subject to greater social control than the other, with both genders being based on genital sex. Lives that do not conform to this dominant pattern are generally treated as human garbage. Breaking apart the forced unity of sex and gender, while increasing the scope of livable lives, is an important goal of transgender feminism and social justice activism.

Gender role: An increasingly outdated term in contemporary society, but one that nevertheless continues to surface in pernicious ways, "gender role" refers to social expectations of proper behavior and activities for a member of a particular gender. It's where stereotypes come from. It is the social script that says a man should be a doctor and a woman should be a nurse, that a woman should be a flight attendant and a man should be a pilot, that mothers should stay at home with their children and fathers should have steady jobs outside the home. While it is certainly possible to live a happy and fulfilled life by choosing to do things that are socially conventional (such as being a stay-at-home mom), gender roles tell us that if we don't perform the prescribed expectations, we are failing to be proper women or men.

Gender comportment: We perform our social gender through our gender comportment, bodily actions such as how we use our voices, cross our legs, hold our heads, wear our clothes, dance around the room, throw a ball, walk in high heels. These are things that each of us learns to do during the course of our lives by watching and mirroring others with whom we identify, as well as by being subtly (or not so subtly) disciplined by other members of our society (particularly by our families) when we perform the "wrong" thing or perform the "right" thing poorly.

Gender identity: Each person has a subjective sense of fit with a particular gender category; this is one's gender identity. For most people, there is a sense of congruence between the category one has been assigned to and trained in, and what one considers oneself to be. Transgender people demonstrate that this is not always the case—that it is possible to form a sense of oneself as *not like* other members of the gender one has been assigned to, or to think of oneself as properly belonging to another gender category. Many people who have never experienced a sense of gender incongruence doubt that transgender people can really experience this, and transgender people who experience it often have a hard time explaining to others what this feels like. One's gender identity could perhaps best be described as how one feels about being referred to by a particular pronoun. How gender identity develops in the first place and how gender identities can be so diverse are hotly debated topics that go straight into the controversies about nature versus nurture and biological determinism versus cultural construction. Some people think that transgender feelings are caused by inborn physical characteristics; others think that they are caused by how children are raised or by the emotional dynamics in their families.

Gender identity disorder: Feelings of unhappiness or distress about the incongruence between the gender-signifying parts of one's body, one's gender identity, and one's social gender (a condition sometimes called "gender dysphoria") are officially classified by medical and psychiatric professionals in the United States as a mental illness known as Gender Identity Disorder, or GID. GID is very controversial within transgender communities. Some people resent having their sense of gender labeled as a sickness, while others take great comfort from believing they have a condition that can be cured with proper treatment. Generally, a person who wants to use hormones and surgery to change his or her gender appearance, or who wants to change his or her legal or bureaucratic sex, has to be diagnosed with GID. This requires a psychological evaluation and a period of living in the desired gender role before access is granted

Gender Identity Disorder

The *Diagnostic and Statistical Manual of Mental Disorders, Fourth Edition*, published in 2000, includes the following diagnostic criteria for gender identity disorder.

302.6 Gender Identity Disorder in Children
302.85 Gender Identity Disorder in Adolescents or Adults

A. A strong and persistent cross-gender identification (not merely a desire for any perceived cultural advantages of being the other sex). In children, the disturbance is manifested by four (or more) of the following:
(1) repeatedly stated desire to be, or insistence that he or she is, the other sex;
(2) in boys, preference for cross-dressing or simulating female attire; in girls, insistence on wearing only stereotypical masculine clothing;
(3) strong and persistent preferences for cross-sex roles in make-believe play or persistent fantasies of being the other sex;
(4) intense desire to participate in the stereotypical games and pastimes of the other sex;
(5) strong preference for playmates of the other sex. In adolescents and adults, the disturbance is manifested by symptoms such as a stated desire to be the other sex, frequent passing as the other sex, desire to live or be treated as the other sex, or the conviction that he or she has the typical feelings and reactions of the other sex.

to medical treatments, which then allow for a legal change in gender status. Some transgender people question why gender change needs to be medicalized in the first place, while others argue that they should have access to healthcare services without having their need to do so be considered pathological. In spite of its being an official psychopathology, "treatments" for GID are not covered by health insurance in the United States because they are considered "elective,"

*B. Persistent discomfort with his or her sex or sense of inappropriate-
ness in the gender role of that sex. In children, the disturbance is manifested by any of the following: in boys, assertion that his penis or testes
are disgusting or will disappear or assertion that it would be better not
to have a penis, or aversion toward rough-and-tumble play and rejection of male stereotypical toys, games, and activities; in girls, rejection
of urinating in a sitting position, assertion that she has or will grow a
penis, or assertion that she does not want to grow breasts or menstru-
ate, or marked aversion toward normative feminine clothing. In adolescents and adults, the disturbance is manifested by symptoms such as
preoccupation with getting rid of primary and secondary sex characteristics (e.g., request for hormones, surgery, or other procedures to physically alter sexual characteristics to simulate the other sex) or belief that
he or she was born the wrong sex.*

C. The disturbance is not concurrent with a physical intersex condition.

*D. The disturbance causes clinically significant distress or impairment
in social, occupational, or other important areas of functioning.*

Specify if (for sexually mature individuals):
Sexually Attracted to Males
Sexually Attracted to Females
Sexually Attracted to Both
Sexually Attracted to Neither

"cosmetic," or even "experimental." This is a truly inexcusable double
bind—if being transgendered is not considered psychopathological,
it should be delisted as a mental disorder; if it is to be considered
psychopathological, its treatment should be covered as a legitimate
healthcare need. The status of GID and the rationale for transgender
access to healthcare raise important questions about the U.S. healthcare
industry more generally, and about the increasingly powerful ways that

medicine and science define our bodies and lives. Struggles revolving around GID form an important part of transgender political history and contemporary activism.

Sexuality: What we find erotic and how we take pleasure in our bodies constitute our sexuality. For most of us, this involves using our sex organs (genitals), but sexuality can involve many body parts or physical activities, as well as the erotic use of objects. Sexuality describes how (and with whom) we act on our erotic desires. Sexuality is analytically distinct from gender but intimately bound with it, like two lines on a graph that have to intersect. The most common terms we use to label or classify our erotic desires depend on identifying the gender of the person toward whom our desire is directed: "heterosexual" (toward a member of another gender), "homosexual" (toward a member of the same gender), "bisexual" (toward a member of any gender). These terms also depend on our understanding of our own gender—*homo-* and *hetero-* make sense only in relation to a gender they are the "same as" or "different from." We can also be "asexual" (not expressing erotic desire for anyone) or "autosexual" (taking pleasure in our own bodies rather than in interacting with others). Because many transgender people don't fit into other people's sexual orientation categories (or because they don't have a clear sense themselves of where they might fit in), there is a relatively high proportion of asexuality and autosexuality in transgender populations. Some people are specifically attracted to transgender people. A transgender person may be of any sexual orientation, just like a nontransgender person.

Transvestite: This is an old word, coined in 1910 by the German sexologist Magnus Hirschfeld. He used it to describe "the erotic urge for disguise," which is how he understood the motivation that led some people to wear clothing generally associated with a social gender other than the one assigned to them at birth. For Hirschfeld, "transvestites" were one of many different types of "sexual intermediaries," including homosexuals and hermaphrodites, who occupied a spectrum between "pure male" and "pure female." Initially, this term was used in much the way that "transgender" (see below) is used now, to convey the sense of a wide range of gender-variant identities and behaviors. During the course of the last century, however, to the extent that it has not fallen entirely out of favor, it refers primarily to people who wear gender-atypical clothing but do not engage in other kinds of body modification. It usually refers to men rather than women and usually carries with it the association of cross-dressing for erotic pleasure.

SOMETHING LIKE A BROTHER

FLORA: "What a very pretty waistcoat, Emily!"

EMILY: "Yes, dear. It belongs to my brother Charles. When he goes out of town, he puts me on the Free List, as he calls it, of his wardrobe. Isn't it kind?"

Popular opinion in the nineteenth century sometimes linked feminist dress reform activism with cross-gender dressing.

Cross-dresser: A term intended as a nonjudgmental replacement for "transvestite," it is usually considered to be neutrally descriptive of the practice of wearing gender-atypical clothing rather than associating that practice with an erotic impulse. The practice of cross-dressing can have many meanings and motivations: Besides being a way to resist or move away from an assigned social gender, it could be a theatrical practice (either comic or dramatic), part of fashion or politics (such as the practice of women's wearing pants once was), part of religious ceremonies, or part of celebrating public festivals and holidays (such as Mardi Gras, Carnival, or Halloween).

Transsexual: Another term sometimes traced to Magnus Hirschfeld, it typically refers to people who feel a strong desire to change their sexual morphology in order to live entirely as permanent, full-time members of the gender other than the one they were assigned to at birth. The term was used in the title of a 1949 article by D. O. Caldwell, "Psychopathia Transexualis," but it was popularized by Dr. Harry Benjamin in the 1950s and became widely known as a result of the spectacular publicity given to the 1952 surgical "sex change" of Christine Jorgensen, a former photographer and film editor from the Bronx whose genital conversion operation made headlines around the world. The term "transsexual" was introduced to draw a distinction between those "transvestites" who sought medical interventions to change their physical bodies (that is, their "sex") and those who merely wanted to change their gendered clothing (the "vestments" in the root of "transvestite"). Historically, the practice of transsexuality has involved surgical modification of the reproductive organs and chest, hormone use to change secondary sex characteristics, and permanent removal of facial and body hair for individuals moving from male embodiment toward social womanhood. These medical procedures have then been the basis for legal or bureaucratic changes in gender designation. More recently, people who don't consider themselves to be transsexual have increasingly started using these same body modification practices, and they may do so without trying to change their legal gender. (For example, a person born with a female body might use testosterone or have mastectomies but still live legally or socially as a woman with traditionally masculine attributes). The result of such practices is another layer of human-generated complexity added on top of already complicated biological sex differences and cultural gender categories. The breakdown in familiar distinctions between who is a transsexual and who is not, and who (based on diagnosis with GID) is considered an acceptable recipient of medicalized body modification procedures, is another very hotly debated topic. The rapid evolution of new motives for changing one's embodiment (for example, a woman with a known genetic risk for breast cancer opting for a "preventive" mastectomy, or a professional athlete taking performance-enhancing drugs—neither of whom may consider themselves transgendered, but who do some of the same things to their bodies that transgender people do to theirs), coupled with new biomedical possibilities for doing so, is part of what drives the rapidly developing terminology in the transgender field.

Transgender: The key term around which this book revolves, "transgender" has become widespread only in the last decade, although the word has a longer history (which will be discussed in later chapters). As noted at the beginning of this chapter, the term implies movement away from an initially assigned gender position. It most generally refers to any and all kinds of variation from gender norms and expectations. Of course, given that all gender, as defined above, varies through place and time, defining "transgender" in this way inevitably brings up the related questions of "Which norms and expectations?" and "Whose norms and expectations?" What counts as *trans*gender varies as much as gender itself, and it always depends on historical and cultural context. It seems safe to say that the difference between gender and transgender in any given situation, however, involves the difference between a dominant or common construction of gender and a marginalized or infrequent one. Recently, some people have begun to use the term "transgender" to refer *only* to those who identify with a gender other than the one they were assigned to at birth, and to use other terms for people who seek to resist their birth-assigned gender without abandoning it, or who seek to create some kind of new gender location. This book uses "transgender" to refer to the widest imaginable range of gender-variant practices and identities.

Transman or transwoman: In transgender communities, people commonly use the words "transmen," "transgender men," or "transsexual men" when they are talking about people who were born with female bodies but consider themselves to be men and live socially as men. Likewise, the words "transwomen," "transgender women," or "transsexual women" refer to people born with male bodies who consider themselves to be women and live socially as women. The "man" and "woman" refer, in keeping with the definition of gender given above, to the social category the person belongs to, not his or her original biological sex. Pronoun use similarly refers to social gender and gender identity: "she" and "her" are appropriate for transgender women, and "he" and "him" for transgender men. In a lot of medical literature, especially older literature, the reverse is often true. Doctors and psychiatrists tend to use "transsexual male" to refer to transgender women (and will often say "he") and "transsexual female" to refer to transgender men (and often say "she"). In keeping with more general social etiquette, it's considered polite to use the gender terms preferred by the person to whom they refer.

Genderqueer: In the early 1990s, some people started to use the word "queer," which had been a derogatory term for homosexuality, in a positive way. Although it's now often used as a synonym for gay or lesbian, the people who first reappropriated the term were trying to find a way to talk about their opposition to heterosexual social norms without automatically assuming that meant they were gay; "queer" was less a sexual orientation than it was a political one, what the "queer theorists" of the day called being "antiheteronormative" (a term discussed more fully in chapter 5). "Queer" is usually associated with sexuality, but from the beginning a vocal minority insisted on the importance of transgender and gender-variant practices for queer politics. Many such people took to calling themselves "genderqueers." People who use "transgender" to refer only to those kinds of people who want to live in a gender other than the one assigned to them at birth sometimes use "genderqueer" to mean the kinds of people who resist gender norms without "changing sex," but this is not always the case.

Alphabet soup: A lot of acronyms are used by members of the T section of the LGBTIQQA (lesbian, gay, bisexual, transgender, intersex, queer, questioning, and allies) community. MTF and FTM refer, respectively, to "male-to-female" and "female-to-male," indicating the direction of gender crossing; it would be more accurate to talk about "male-to-woman" or "female-to-man," but the fact of the matter is that nobody actually says those things. (Some transgender people resent and resist these "directional" labels, claiming they make about as much sense as calling someone a "heterosexual-to-gay" man or "heterosexual-to-lesbian" woman, and that they serve only to marginalize transmen and transwomen within the larger populations of other men and women.) CD (or sometimes XD) means "cross-dressing." TS refers to a transsexual, who might be pre-op or post-op, or even no-ho /no-op (electing neither hormones nor surgery but still identifying as a member of the gender he or she was not assigned to at birth). A TG is "a transgender," which, when used as an identity label rather than a broadly descriptive term, often refers to those who live permanently in a social gender they were not assigned to at birth, might or might not use hormones, might or might not have chest surgery, but who usually don't have genital surgery. The right term to use in reference to any particular person really isn't in the eye of the beholder—it's determined by the person who applies it to him-, her-, or itself.

Gender-neutral pronouns: Given that the English language doesn't allow us to refer to other individuals without gendering them (we have to choose between "he," "she," or "it," with the latter not considered appropriate for reference to humans precisely because it doesn't indicate a gender), some transgender people favor the use of newly coined, "gender-neutral" pronouns. They might use "ze" or "sie" in place of "he" or "she," or the word "hir" instead of "his" or "her." Sometimes, in writing, people will use the unpronounceable "s/he." Appropriate use of gender-neutral pronouns can be tricky. The practice often works well within transgender communities, where many people understand what's being said, but it can get confusing for outsiders. Changes in language structure usually happen very slowly and pronouns are among the linguistic elements most resistant to change, so trying to speed up a change of usage can sometimes sound forced or strange. Some transgender people—often those who have worked very hard to attain a gender status other than the one assigned to them at birth—take offense when gender-neutral pronouns, rather than the appropriate gendered ones, are applied to them because they perceive this usage as a way that others fail to acknowledge their attained gender.

Cisgender or cissexual: Two other recently coined words that are gaining a following are "cisgender" and "cissexual," which some people prefer to the words "nontransgendered" or "nontranssexual." The prefix *cis-* means "on the same side as" (that is, the opposite of *trans*). The idea behind the terms is to resist the way that "woman" or "man" can mean "nontransgendered woman" or "nontransgendered man" by default, unless the person's transgender status is explicitly named; it's the same logic that would lead somebody to prefer saying "white woman" and "black woman" rather than simply using "woman" to describe a white woman (thus presenting white as the norm) and "black woman" to indicate a deviation from the norm. Similarly, "cisgendered" or "cissexual" names the usually unstated assumption of nontransgender status contained in the words "man" and "woman."

Subcultural terms: In an important sense, all the terms mentioned in this section on definitions are subcultural terms—words that originate and circulate within a smaller subset of a larger culture. However, the terms listed here are also the ones most often used by cultural elites, or within mass media, or within powerful professions such as science and medicine and academia. They are often derived from the experiences of white transgender people. But there are hundreds, if not thousands, of other specialized words related to the subject matter of this book that could just as easily be listed in this section on terms and definitions. A number of these words come out of gay and lesbian subcultures—for example, "drag" (clothing associated with a particular gender or activity, often worn in a parodic, self-conscious, or theatrical manner); "drag king" and "drag queen" (people who engage in cross-gender performance, either on the stage or on the street, usually in subcultural spaces such as gay-friendly bars, nightclubs, neighborhoods, or commercial sex zones); "butch" (the expression of traits, mannerisms, or appearances usually associated with masculinity, particularly when expressed by lesbian women or gay men); or "femme" (the expression of traits, mannerisms, or appearances usually associated with femininity, particularly when expressed by lesbian women or gay men). Many terms, such as "bulldagger" for a very butch woman, originate in queer communities of color. The "house" subcultures of many urban African American, Latino, and Asian American communities (such as the ones represented in Jennie Livingston's film *Paris Is Burning*) have large costume balls in which participants "walk the categories," competing for best enactment of a multitude of very highly stylized gender categories. Some words referring to practices or identities that are termed "transgender" in this book are culturally or ethnically specific, such as the *hijra* in India, the Polynesian *mahu*, South American *travesti,* or Native American "two-spirit." The seemingly inexhaustible global catalog of specialized terms for gender variety shows how impossible it really is to group such a wide range of phenomena together under the single term "transgender" without keeping that word's definition very flexible and without paying close attention to who is using it to refer to whom, and for what reasons.

A final note on the use of the words "queer" and "transgender" throughout the text: Oddly enough, for somebody trained as a historian, I sometimes use these words in ways that may sound anachronistic. One reason for doing so is simply stylistic—they are short, easily pronounced, familiar words that can serve as a shorthand for a more complicated idea or identity or way of acting that would be cumbersome to spell out in detail. But the other reason has to do with the kind of intellectual work that I want these words to do. Sometimes I use "queer" to describe many different kinds of people who come together in the same space or for a common cause—for example, to protest discrimination aimed at drag queens at Compton's Cafeteria in 1966 (described in chapter 3)—because I don't want to say "gay, lesbian, bisexual, transgender, drag, and butch individuals, along with male and female prostitutes who might well be heterosexual" every time I need to refer to the group collectively. The idea I'm trying to get across is that many different kinds of people might in fact have something in common with one another in their opposition to an oppressive situation. I also want to avoid heading down the rabbit hole of historical nit-picking. All of these terms have their histories, which can bog down the storytelling, unless telling those histories is the point of the story. So I have chosen, in some instances, to just use the word "queer" rather than split hairs about precisely which term would be most accurate at any particular time and place.

Likewise, I use the word "transgender" as a shorthand way of talking about a wide range of gender variance and gender atypicality in periods before the word was coined, and I sometimes apply it to people who might not apply it to themselves. Some butch women or queeny men will say that they are not transgender because they do not want to change sex. Some transsexuals will say that they are not transgender because they do. There is no way of using the word that doesn't offend some people by including them where they don't want to be included or excluding them from where they do want to be included. And yet, I still think the term is useful as a simple word for indicating when some practice or identity crosses gender boundaries that are considered socially normative in the contemporary United States. Calling all of these things transgender is a device for telling a story about the political history of gender variance that is not limited to any one particular experience.

Transgender Issues in the Spotlight

Why the current obsession with all things transgender, when transgender phenomena seem to be a pretty persistent part of human cultures across time and around the world? Although the mass media have paid nonstop attention to transgender issues since at least the 1950s, the past several years certainly have witnessed a steady increase in transgender visibility, and the trend has been toward increasingly positive representation. As of late 2007, Googling "transgender" retrieves roughly 7.3 million hits, while "transsexual" nets 6.4 million, "transvestite" gets 3.1 million, and "drag queen" gets 1.9 million ("drag king" results in only about 200,000 hits, roughly the same as "genderqueer"). Back in the 1950s, Christine Jorgensen could generate millions of words of press coverage simply for *being* transsexual, whereas now the contemporary media are completely saturated with continual references to and representations of transsexuality and other transgender phenomena—everything from a teacher who changes sex on the animated cable television show *South Park* to a Barbara Walters newsmagazine report on children who transition at an early age to a segment of *Larry King Live* devoted to "Transgender World" to a *Newsweek* cover story on transgenderism. What's all the fuss about?

The contingency of gender, mentioned above, has to be taken into consideration when answering that question—a lot of cultural trends, social conditions, and historical circumstances have collided to make "transgender" a hot topic. Some people think that the numbers of transgender people are on the rise. Those who favor biological theories point to environmental factors. Other observers insist that increased transgender visibility is just an artifact of the Internet age—not really a rise in prevalence, just a new way for previously isolated and socially invisible people to link up and disseminate information about themselves. Still others, of a particular religious frame of mind, are keen to interpret rampant transgenderism as a token of the moral debauchery they believe will characterize the last days of humanity on earth before the Apocalypse.

The more secular minded point to the confluence of several other contributing factors. Globalization brings us all into increasingly frequent and extensive contact with people from cultures different from our own—including people who have different experiences of gender and sexuality. Among many politically progressive people, an emerging transnational perspective has sensitized those of us who live in the United States to be more aware of how our foundational assumptions about what the world is like are just that—assumptions, and not always true for other people. In feminist and gay movements, this trend has led some people to rethink how feminist and gay politics can unwittingly reproduce gender norms. As a result, transgender issues, which call our attention to otherwise invisible complexities of the gender system's operation, have come to be seen as cutting-edge concerns for some gays, lesbians, and feminists. Sociologically, transgender communities have been coming into closer and closer alignment with sexual minority communities. This is due in part to the AIDS/HIV epidemic that began in the 1980s (male-to-female transsexuals of color have one of the highest infection rates of any population in the world) and in part to the queer movement in the 1990s, which worked to break down old divisions between sexual identity communities. It's precisely because transgender phenomena provide meaty evidence for contemporary debates about identity and community that transgender issues have become an increasingly studied topic in the humanities and social sciences.

The current fascination with transgender also probably has something to do with new ideas about how representation works in the age of digital media. Back in the analog era, a representation (word, image, idea) was commonly assumed to point to some real thing, the same way a photograph was an image produced by light bouncing off a physical object and causing a chemical change on a piece of paper, or the way a sound recording was a groove cut in a piece of vinyl by sound waves produced by a musical instrument or a person's voice. A person's social and psychological gender was commonly assumed to point to that person's biological sex in exactly the same way: Gender was considered a representation of a physical sex. But a digital image or sound is something else entirely. It's unclear exactly how it's related to the world of physical objects. It doesn't point to some "real" thing in quite the same way, and it might in fact be a complete fabrication built up pixel by pixel or bit by bit—but a fabrication that nevertheless exists as an image or a sound as real as any other. Transgender gender representation works the same

Religion and Transgender

The Bible says a lot of things about sexuality and gender that even observant Christians and Jews no longer pay much attention to—for example, that if a married couple has intercourse during the woman's menstrual period, both partners should be executed (Leviticus 18:19), or that if a man gets into a fight with another man, and his wife tries to help him out by grabbing the other man's genitals, her hand should be cut off (Deuteronomy 25:11–12). But many people who look for religious justification for their antitransgender views still point to the following verse, Deuteronomy 22:5: "A woman shall not wear man's clothing, nor shall a man put on a woman's clothing; for whoever does these things is an abomination to the Lord your God."

As transgender religious scholar Virginia Ramey Mollenkott points out in *Omnigender*, her award-winning overview of religious attitudes toward sex/gender variance, many Christian fundamentalists have a deep stake in maintaining the gender binary. Right-wing evangelist Charles Colson, for example (who served time in federal prison as one of the conspirators in the Watergate scandal that brought down President Richard Nixon, and whose "born-again" experience there inspired him to launch a prison ministry), has claimed that intersex babies, born with ambiguous genitalia, must undergo surgery to become unambiguously male or female because all individuals have a duty "to be fruitful and multiply," because sexual activity is permissible only within marriage, and because marriage is legally limited to an exchange of vows between one man and one woman.

As Mollenkott's book makes clear, however, many religious traditions, including many denominations and schools of thought within Christianity, adhere to a more tolerant perspective on transgender issues. One organization that promotes acceptance of gender diversity rather than condemnation is the Center for Lesbian and Gay Studies in Religion and the Ministry at the Pacific School of Religion in Berkeley, California (http://clgs. org). The center sponsored a national Transgender Religious Summit in 2007, attracting religiously observant transgender people, ministers, and allies from all around the country.

way. For the generation that's grown up amid the turn-of-the-century digital media and telecommunications revolution, transgender often just makes sense intuitively. It's not as big a deal as it used to be, especially in the big coastal cities, and thus more people who feel led to follow the transgender path do so, with fewer bad consequences.

Probably half a dozen other things also figure into the equation. The end of the Cold War ushered in an era when it became politically imperative to think outside familiar binaries. It's not just East versus West, communism versus capitalism anymore (however much the right wing tries to create new dichotomies between Islam and the West); transgender reflects a similar shift in thinking beyond the binaries of "man" and "woman." There was also that sense in the 1990s, so hard to remember less than a decade later, that the calendar's millennial rollover into the twenty-first century meant we would soon be living in "the future," when everything would be different. Transgender came to represent part of that future, where new biotechnology and medical science promised to turn us all into human-machine hybrids.

But the reality, quite apart from science fiction fantasies, is that biomedical technology really is fundamentally transforming the conditions of human life on earth. Stop for a moment to reflect on recent developments in reproductive technology: cloning, in vitro fertilization, intrauterine surgeries, sperm and egg banking, neonatal critical care, surrogacy, genetic engineering, gene therapy. As these and other biomedical developments continue to coalesce, it appears that we are on the verge of completely separating biological reproduction (the functional reason for sexual difference) from the status of one's social and psychological gender. That is a future radically different from the whole of past human experience. Contemporary transgender issues offer a window onto that coming world.

On a Personal Note . . .

On a gloriously sunny and unseasonably warm San Francisco afternoon in June 2007, Lynnee Breedlove was onstage and working the crowd gathered in Dolores Park at the Fourth Annual Trans March and

Rally—supposedly the largest public gathering to date of transgender people, and friends, allies, supporters, lovers, and families. "How do you tell the trannies from the genderqueers?" asked the former lead singer of the legendary lesbian punk band Tribe 8 and author of the drug-fueled bike messenger cult-novel-cum-underground movie *Godspeed*. Breedlove waited a beat before delivering his punch line: "When you ask the trannies if they're a boy or girl, they answer 'yes'; when you ask the genderqueers, they answer 'no.'"

Lynnee's joke was right on the money, I thought, as I waited backstage to go on and say a few words myself, and as I looked out over the sea of several thousand faces. Even after being in the transgender scene for so long, I found the crowd a bewitching spectacle: brilliantly tattooed, biologically female queer femme women and the trans guys who used to be their dyke girlfriends; straight-looking male-to-female transsexuals with nail salon manicures sitting side by side with countercultural transsexual women sporting face jewelry, dreadlocks, and thrift-store chic; lithe young people of indeterminate gender; black bulldaggers, white fairies, Asian queens, Native two-spirits; effeminate trannyfags and butch transsexual lesbians; kids of parents who had changed sex and parents who supported their kids' rejection of the labels their society had handed them. Some people walked around in fetish gear, some in chain-store khakis or floral-print sundresses from the discount clothing outlet; most wore the casually androgynous style of clothing that is the cultural norm. *Vive la différence*, I thought as I stepped up to the mike and surveyed the beautiful range of human diversity spread out on the grass before me. *Live and let live.*

CHAPTER 2

A HUNDRED YEARS OF TRANSGENDER HISTORY

IMAGINE BEING A YOUNG FEMALE PERSON in the 1850s who can't face a life of marriage and child rearing, who has no practical work skills outside the home, and who dreams of adventure in the military, at sea, or in the mining towns of the mountainous and desert West. Donning your brother's clothes, you slip away in the night and head out to meet your fate. Your life might depend on being taken for exactly what you present yourself to be. Or imagine being a young male person with a fondness for the social companionship of women but no romantic interest in them, whose greatest happiness is in taking care of children. You thrill at the thought of being related to as a woman. You disappear into the streets of a large city, looking for a way of living that feels right to you, but find yourself subjected to all of the indignities that society can visit upon an individual who is feminine, unattached, and unlikely to be offered a job or a home.

Regulating Sexuality and Gender

The transgender movement for social change that emerged in the United States after World War II traces its roots to conditions that began taking shape about a century earlier. Starting in the 1850s, a number of U.S. cities began passing municipal ordinances that made it illegal for a man or woman to appear in public "in a dress not belonging to his or her sex." There's an even longer history of public regulation of dress—dating to the colonial period, ordinances have forbidden people from disguising themselves in public or wearing clothes associated with

Outlawing Cross-Dressing

One of several anti-cross-dressing laws passed in the middle of the nineteenth century, the following San Francisco ordinance was enacted in 1863:

> If any person shall appear in a public place in a state of nudity, or in a dress not belonging to his or her sex, or in an indecent or lewd dress, or shall make any indecent exposure of his or her person, or be guilty of any lewd or indecent act or behavior, or shall exhibit or perform any indecent, immoral or lewd play, or other representation, he should be guilty of a misdemeanor, and on conviction, shall pay a fine not exceeding five hundred dollars.

Municipal Laws Prohibiting Wearing Dress of Opposite Sex

Nineteenth Century			
Location	**Year**	**Location**	**Year**
Columbus Ohio	1848	Dallas, Texas	1880
Chicago, Illinois	1851	Nashville, Tennessee	1881
Wilmington, Delaware	1856	San Jose, California	1882
Springfield, Illinois	1856	Tucson, Arizona	1883
Newark, New Jersey	1858	Columbia, Missouri	1883
Charleston, South Carolina	1858	Peoria, Illinois	1884
Kansas City, Missouri	1860 1889	Butte, Montana	1885
Houston, Texas	1861	Denver, Colorados	1886
Toledo, Ohio	1862	Lincoln, Nebraska	1889
Memphis, Tennessee	1863	Santa Barbara, California	189?
San Francisco, California	1863	Omaha, Nebraska	1890
St. Louis, Missouri	1864	Cheyenne, Wyoming	1892
Minneapolis, Minnesota	1877	Cicero, Illinois	1897
Oakland, California	1879	Cedar Falls, Iowa	1899

Twentieth Century			
Location	**Year**	**Location**	**Year**
Cedar Rapids, Iowa	1906	Pensacola, Florida	1920
Orlando, Florida	1907	Cleveland, Ohio	1924
Wilmington, North Carolina	1913	West palm Beach Florida	1926
Charleston, West Virginia	1913	Detroit, Michigan	195?
Columbus, Georgia	1914	Miami, Florida	1952
			1956
Sarasota, Florida	1919	Cincinnati, Ohio	1974

Compiled by Clare Sears in "A Dress Not Belonging to His or Her Sex: Cross-Dressing Law in San Francisco, 1860–1900," PhD dissertation, Sociology Department, University of California—Santa Cruz, 2005, based on data from William Eskridge, Gaylaw: Challenging the Apartheid of the Closet *(Cambridge: Harvard University Press, 1997).*

a particular social rank or profession, and some also have prevented white people from impersonating Indians or black people from impersonating whites—but the wave of local legislation in the 1850s represented a new development specific to gender presentation. We can interpret this as a response to the changing ways that some people lived their lives in cities.

There's very little historical research that helps us explain why cross-dressing became a social issue seemingly in need of regulation in the 1850s, but an old argument about capitalism and gay identity offers some suggestive parallels. According to historian John D'Emilio, modern gay and lesbian communities weren't possible until the middle of the nineteenth century, with the rise of modern industrial cities and their large working-class populations. It wasn't until men could leave tight-knit rural communities, characterized by intimate and interlocking forms of familial and religious surveillance, that they had the opportunity to form different kinds of emotional and erotic bonds with other men. Cities—where the industrial economy created many wage-paying jobs that allowed single men to be independent from their families of origin and live in relative anonymity within masses of other people—provided the crucial social circumstances for gay communities to take shape.

Because women were less able than men to free themselves from the constraints of marriage, childcare, and the care of aging parents, there was not a similar urban lesbian subculture until the twentieth century, when more women were able to support themselves as independent wage earners. The 1920s were a pivotal decade in this shift. For the first time, the urban population in the United States exceeded the rural population; women wielded historically unprecedented political power through the recently acquired right to vote, and Jazz Age sensibilities embraced more expansive ideas of socially acceptable female sexuality. The greater scope of possibility for independent womanhood came to be seen as an important aspect of a new "modern era"; coalescing after the upheavals of World War I, it was characterized by new entertainment technologies (such as motion pictures and sound recordings), modernist styles of art and literature, and electrically illuminated homes and streets (which created more opportunities for nighttime socializing).

The circumstances that supported the development of homosexual social worlds also applied to people who sought different ways to express their sense of gender. Female-bodied people who could successfully pass as men had greater opportunities to travel and find work. Male-bodied people who identified as women had greater opportunities to live as women in cities far removed from the communities where they had grown up. In practice, the distinctions between what we now call "transgender" and "gay" or "lesbian" were not always as meaningful back then as they have since become. Throughout the second half of the nineteenth century and the first half of the twentieth century, homosexual desire and gender variance were often closely associated; one common way of thinking about homosexuality back then was as gender "inversion," in which a man who was attracted to men was thought to be acting like a woman, and a woman who desired women was considered to be acting like a man.

First wave feminism and an increasingly ethnically diverse population were also likely factors that sparked new efforts to regulate public gender variance beginning in the 1850s. First wave feminism is usually defined as the wave of reform that spanned the entire nineteenth century, beginning with late-eighteenth-century calls for female emancipation such as Mary Wollstonecraft's *Vindication of the Rights of Woman* and culminating in the suffrage campaigns that won women in the United States the right to vote in 1919. Dress reform was an important focus of first wave feminist activism; Amelia Bloomer, for example, argued in the 1840s that long skirts and cumbersome undergarments were essentially a form of bondage that dragged women down, and she advocated that women wear pantslike clothing instead. Nineteenth-century antifeminist opinion, which saw in feminism a threatened loss of distinction between men and women, considered dress reform to be tantamount to cross-dressing. On the West Coast, where the California gold rush and subsequent silver strikes attracted

© University of Wisconsin Press

Loreta Janeta Velazquez passed as Confederate soldier Harry Buford in the Civil War.

many trans-Pacific immigrants from Asia, cultural diversity added another element that upset conventional Euro-American assumptions about gender. Gold rush–era newspapers are full of stories about how difficult it was for European Americans to tell Chinese men apart from Chinese women, because they all wore their hair long and dressed in silky pajamalike costumes. To understand the historical conditions for contemporary transgender activism, we thus have to take into account race, class, culture, sexuality, and sexism, and we have to develop an understanding of the ways that U.S. society has fostered conditions of inequality and injustice for people who aren't white, male, heterosexual, and middle class—in addition to understanding the difficulties particularly associated with engaging in transgender practices.

The Social Power of Medicine

One of the most powerful tools for social regulation in this period was the rapid development of medical science. This is not to suggest that modern medicine hasn't saved many lives and greatly improved the quality of life for untold millions of people—it has. But since the end of the eighteenth century, science has gradually come to replace religion as the highest social authority; since the middle of the nineteenth century, medical science has played an increasingly central role in defining everyday life. It has often been used for very conservative social purposes—"proving" that black people are inferior to white people, or that females are inferior to males. Medical practitioners and institutions have the social power to determine what is considered sick or healthy, normal or pathological, sane or insane—and thus, often, to transform potentially neutral forms of human difference into unjust and oppressive social hierarchies. This particular operation of medicine's social power has been particularly important in transgender history.

For those transgender people who have felt compelled to change something about their embodiment, medical science has long offered the prospect of increasingly satisfactory interventions. Once anesthesia had been invented and a new understanding of the importance of antisepsis had made surgery something other than a likely death sentence (once again, in the middle decades of the nineteenth century), individuals began approaching doctors to request surgical alteration of gender-signifying parts of their bodies. But medical science has always been a two-edged sword—its representatives' willingness to intervene has gone hand in hand with their power to define and judge. Far too often, access to medical services for transgender people has depended on constructing transgender phenomena as symptoms of a mental illness or physical malady, partly because "sickness" is the condition that typically legitimizes medical intervention.

It's possible to see medical and psychiatric professionals—as well as people seeking relief from gender-related distress (or simply struggling to define themselves)—groping over the course of the nineteenth century for new words, labels, and identity categories. In Austria, Karl Heinrich Ulrichs anonymously published a series of booklets in 1864–65 under the collective title *Researches on the Riddle of "Man-Manly" Love;* in them he developed a biological theory to account for people such as himself, whom he called "urnings," and whom he described with the Latin phrase *anima muliebris virili corpore inclusa* (meaning "a female soul enclosed within a male body"). It was in correspondence with Ulrichs that the German-born Hungarian citizen Karl Maria Kertbeny first coined the term "homosexual" in 1869, which he also intended to connote same-sex love, minus the element of gender inversion to be found in the term "urning." Both men considered the respective conditions they described to be physical and inborn, and thus proper objects of medical inquiry; Ulrichs and Kertbeny also thought that because transgender/homosexual feelings had a biological basis, laws against their expression should be reformed in the name of a rational social order that reflected scientific truth. Their efforts represent early instances of social activism based on the idea that people we would now probably label gay or transgender were not by definition sinners or criminals but simply different kinds of people who were equally entitled to full participation in society. The logic of their arguments still informs many transgender and gay social justice efforts; more often than not, however, biological theories about gender variance and homosexuality are used to argue that gay and transgender people are physically and psychologically degenerate, and that these conditions therefore should be corrected or eliminated.

Many other long-gone words for transgender phenomena pop up in the burgeoning medical literature of the late nineteenth and early twentieth centuries, demonstrating the extent to which transgender issues were coming to be seen as a medical problem. The period's leading scientific authority on sexuality, Richard von Krafft-Ebing, supplied a great many terms in the several editions of his influential medical compendium, *Psychopathia Sexualis* (first published in 1886). These included "antipathic sexual instinct" (disliking what one *should* find erotic based on one's sex or gender), "eviration" (a deep change of character in which a male's feelings and inclinations become those of a woman), "defemination" (a deep change of character in which a female's feelings and inclinations become those of a man), and "metamorphosis sexualis paranoica" (the psychotic belief that one's body was transforming into the other sex). Krafft-Ebing also wrote about "insanity among the Scythians" (an ancient Mediterranean people who practiced ritual genital modification as part of their religious observations), and about *mujerados,* "male women" noted by the Spanish conquistadors during the colonization of the Americas, whom he believed had become feminized through excessive masturbation, leading to atrophy of the penis and testicles. One early psychiatrist, Albert Moll, wrote about *conträre Geschlechtsempfindung* (contrary sexual feeling) in 1891; another, Max Marcuse, described a *Geschlechtsumwandlungstreib* (drive for sex transformation) in 1913. That same year, British psychologist Havelock Ellis coined "Sexo-Aesthetic Inversion" (wanting to look like the other sex) and later, in 1928, "Eonism," which referred to the Chevalier D'eon, a member of the court of Louis XVI who, at various stages of life, lived alternately as a man and as a woman. It was in this climate of ever-evolving vocabulary and increasing attention to transgender phenomena that Magnus Hirschfeld coined "transvestite" in 1910, the only word of its kind to survive into contemporary usage.

An Early Advocate

Hirschfeld was a pivotal figure in the political history of sexuality and gender. Born in Prussia in 1868, he earned a degree in medicine at the University of Berlin in 1892. His most important theoretical contribution to the study of gender and sexuality was his concept of "sexual intermediaries," the idea that every human being represented a unique combination of sex characteristics, secondary sex-linked traits, erotic preferences, psychological inclinations, and culturally acquired habits and practices. In 1897, he cofounded the Scientific-Humanitarian Committee, usually regarded as the first organization in the world to effectively devote itself to social reform on behalf of sexual minorities. Like Ulrichs and Kertbeny before him, Hirschfeld thought that variations in human sexuality and gender were rooted in biology, and that a just society was one that recognized the natural order of things. Hirschfeld edited the first scientific journal on "sexual variants," the *Yearbook for Sexual Intermediaries,* published between 1899 and 1923, and was a founding member of Sigmund Freud's Vienna Psychoanalytic Society in 1908 (which he broke with in 1911). In 1919, he founded the Institute for Sexual Science in Berlin—a combination of library, archive, lecture hall, and medical clinic, where he amassed an unprecedented collection of historical documents, ethnographies, case studies, and literary works detailing the diversity of sexuality and gender around the world. In 1928, he became the founding president of the World League for Sexual Reform.

Hirschfeld was a pioneering advocate for transgender people. As early as 1910 he had written *The Transvestites,* the first book-length treatment of transgender phenomena. He worked with the Berlin police department to end the harassment and targeting for arrest of transgender people. Transgender people worked on the staff of the Institute for Sexual Science (albeit as receptionists and maids), and some were part of Hirschfeld's social circle as well, including Dora Richter. Richter underwent the first documented male-to-female genital transformation surgery in 1931, arranged on her behalf by Hirschfeld himself. Hirschfeld was the linchpin, and his institute the hub, of the international network of transgender people and progressive medical experts who set the stage for the post–World War II transgender movement. His colleagues included Eugen Steinach, the Austrian endocrinologist who first identified the morphological effects of the so-called "sex hormones," testosterone and estrogen, in the 1910s, as well as young Harry Benjamin, the German-born doctor who moved to the United States in 1913 and became the leading medical authority on transsexuality in the 1950s.

Hirschfeld's work came to an abrupt and tragically premature end in the 1930s. The World League for Sexual Reform splintered between liberal and radical factions (some members favoring the reform politics of Western democratic capitalism, and others favoring Soviet-style Marxist revolution) and had to cancel planned conferences because of the rise of Stalinism and fascism in Europe. Adolf Hitler personally denounced Hirschfeld, who was a socialist as well as a homosexual, as "the most dangerous Jew in Germany." Fearing for his life if he remained in the country, Hirschfeld turned a planned visit to the United States into an around-the-world lecture tour. Between 1930 and 1933 he visited New York, Chicago, San Francisco, Honolulu, the Philippines, Indonesia, Japan, China, Egypt, and Palestine, preaching his vision of politically progressive sexual science. In 1933, fascist vigilantes ransacked and destroyed Hirschfeld's Institute in Berlin—the most familiar photo of Nazi book burning, in fact, depicts Hirschfeld's library of materials on

© National Archives

sexual diversity going up in flames, a bust of Hirschfeld himself clearly visible in the bonfire. Unable to return to Germany, Magnus Hirschfeld settled in Nice, on the French Riviera, where he died on his sixty-seventh birthday, in 1935.

By the early twentieth century, some transgender individuals had also sought the legitimation afforded by science to argue for better social treatment of people such as themselves. One of

Nazis burn the library of Magnus Hirschfeld's Institute for Sexual Science in Berlin, 1933.

the "case studies" for Hirschfeld's 1910 book on transvestites, a German American living in San Francisco, had first come to his attention after writing to a German feminist publication to suggest that mothers should raise their transgender children according to their "mental sex" rather than their "physical sex." Earl Lind, a self-described "androgyne," "hermaphrodite," and "fairy" in New York who also used the name Jennie June, wrote two autobiographical works, *Autobiography of an Androgyne* (1918) and *The Female Impersonators* (1922). The first was aimed at doctors, the second at the general public, but both were intended to "help the suffering androgyne"; the books' publisher, Dr. Alfred Herzog, likewise said he brought them into print because "androgynism was not sufficiently understood" and "therefore androgynes were unjustly made to suffer." According to Lind, a group of New York androgynes led by one Roland Reeves had formed "a little club" called The Cercle Hermaphroditos as early as 1895, based on their self-perceived need "to unite for defense against the world's bitter persecution."

Midcentury Transgender Social Networks

The Cercle Hermaphroditos was the first known organization in the United States to concern itself with what we might now call transgender social justice issues, but it does not appear to have had any lasting influence or inspired any direct successors. Not until the middle of the twentieth century did social networks of transgender people begin to interconnect with networks of socially powerful people in ways that would produce long-lasting organizations and provide the base of a social movement.

The staff and clients of the Langley Porter Psychiatric Clinic at the University of California—San Francisco (UCSF) played an important role in this transformation. Under the direction of Karl Bowman, a former president of the American Psychiatric Association, the Langley Porter Clinic became a major center of research on variant sexuality and gender in the 1940s and '50s—in sometimes ominous ways. During World War II, Bowman conducted research on homosexuality in the military, using as test subjects gay men whose sexuality had been

Case 13: The Story of a Nineteenth-Century

In Magnus Hirschfeld's *The Transvestites*, "Case 13" consists of letters, written in 1909, from a person known variously as Jenny, Johanna, and John, who was born in the Austro-Hungarian Empire and later moved to the United States. Hirschfeld considered this person to be "a typical representative of the group we are concerned with." These reminiscences are abridged from the original.

> *I was born in 1862. I did not want any trousers and put up such a fuss, and since my sister was one year older I could wear her clothes until Mother died in 1868. My aunts then forced me to wear boys clothing. I clearly remember that I always only wanted to be a girl, and my relatives and acquaintances would tease me.*
>
> *I wanted to go to the teachers' seminary, because later, I thought, when I finished, I could go around as a governess or a children's teacher. Even at the time I had firm plans to become a woman. When I saw that they were not going to allow me to study to be a teacher, at the first opportunity I stole from a girl who was my size. I put on her things and took her certificate of domicile and burned my boy's things that night. Everything boyish I left behind and went to Switzerland where my relatives would not know where I was.*
>
> *I first went to work as a nanny and did general housework. At the same time I learned embroidery. I grew strong and not ugly, so that boys would lie in wait for me. At that time I felt fully a young woman, except when the fellows got fresh with me, and it would occur to me that, unfortunately, I was not one.*

discovered while they were serving in uniform, and who were being held in a military psychiatric prison at the Treasure Island Naval Base in San Francisco Bay. After the war, he was the principal investigator for a statewide project funded by the California Sex Deviates Research Act of 1950 to discover the "causes and cures" of homosexuality; part of this research involved castrating male sex offenders in California prisons and experimenting on them by administering various sex hormones to see if it altered their sexual behavior.

"Transvestite"

At 16 1/2 a man tried to rape me. I protected myself, but he gave me a bad name as being a hermaphrodite, so I had to move away and went to France. I had a friendship with a girl, who, like me, was in opposition to her sex, namely manly, and when she went to St. Quentin to the embroidery factory there, I followed her. There I had the opportunity for the first time to come together with women who with other women lived like married people.

In 1882 I left France and went to New York. Here, I soon found work as a maid on a farm because I thought I would be able to live there inconspicuously, but one day the farmer's wife was away and he became fresh. I was afraid of discovery and left that place and got a good job in Jersey City.

I became acquainted with an embroiderer who found out I was no young woman. He threatened to call the police and tell them I was playing a masquerade. He forced me into sodomy and fellatio and a few months passed during which I got more miserable each day. One morning I packed everything together and, when he was away, sold everything of worth. I went to Montana as a woman cook. There, however, betrayed again, I took myself to San Francisco in 1885, and still live there today.

I am now 47 years old and today it is still my deepest wish to wear a new princess dress, a new flowered hat, and lace petticoats. I decorate my bedroom in the manner of women, and a man seldom enters my room, because I am no friend to men. Conversations with women satisfy me more, and I am envious of educated women, because I look up to them. For that reason I have always been an activist for equal rights.

In the course of this work, Bowman became acquainted with several individuals living in San Francisco whom we would now call transsexuals, as he noted in his first report to the California State Legislature:

I have records of two males, both of whom have asked for complete castration, including amputation of the penis, construction of an artificial vagina, and the administration

> *of female sex hormones. I also have two cases of females who have requested a panhysterectomy and the amputation of their breasts, together with the giving of male sex hormones, in the hope that in some way the clitoris may finally develop into a penis. Male homosexuals of this type are called "Queens" and seem to differ markedly from the main group of homosexuals who are more nearly like the average man. Here we have an extremely interesting field for further investigation. We are therefore setting up a careful plan to study a group of these so-called "Queens."*

One of the transgender people Bowman came in contact with (though not one of the prospective transsexuals) was Louise Lawrence, a biological male who began living full-time as a woman in 1942. Lawrence, a native of Northern California who had been cross-dressing most of her life, had developed an extensive correspondence network with transgender people around the world by placing personal ads in magazines, and by contacting people whose arrests for public cross-dressing had been covered in the newspapers. Lawrence frequently lectured on transgender topics to Bowman's colleagues at UCSF.

Lawrence's connections to Bowman, and through him to other sex researchers such as the famed Alfred Kinsey, functioned as a crucial interface between medical researchers and transgender social networks. Her home became a way station for transgender people from across the country who sought access to medical procedures in San Francisco, and her numerous transgender contacts supplied the data that a new generation of sex researchers would use to formulate their theories. In 1949, Bowman and Kinsey, along with transsexual medical pioneer Harry Benjamin and future California governor Edmund G. (Pat) Brown (then California's state attorney general), became involved in a legal case involving one of Lawrence's friends that had long-lasting repercussions for the course of transgender access to medical services in the United States. Brown, on the advice of Bowman and Kinsey but over the objections of Benjamin, offered the legal opinion that transsexual genital modification would constitute "mayhem" (the willful destruction of healthy tissue) and would expose any surgeon who performed such an operation to possible criminal prosecution. That opinion cast a pall, lasting for years, over efforts by U.S. transgender people to gain access to transsexual medical procedures in their own country. In the 1950s, only a few dozen "sex change" operations were performed in the United States, most of them by Los Angeles urologist Elmer Belt (a friend of Benjamin's), under conditions of secrecy.

Pioneering transgender community organizer Louise Lawrence.

© Oviatt Library, Cal State Northridge

This 1949 "mayhem" case was notable in one further regard: It was Harry Benjamin's first involving a transsexual patient. The case thus helps link the emerging transgender scene in the United States with the earlier one in Europe that revolved around Magnus Hirschfeld. Benjamin was born in Berlin in 1885 and earned his medical doctorate at the University of Tübigen in 1912. He had become acquainted with Hirschfeld through a mutual friend in 1907, and he had accompanied Hirschfeld on trips into Berlin's transvestite nightclub subculture, but at the time Benjamin's professional interest was in tuberculosis. In the 1920s, after Benjamin had taken up residence in New York, he developed an interest in the new science of endocrinology. He became a devotee of an Austrian pioneer in the field, Hirschfeld's colleague Eugen Steinach, and visited the two men every summer in Vienna and Berlin to learn more about the use of hormones as a life-extension and geriatric rejuvenation therapy. Benjamin, who organized the U.S. leg of Hirschfeld's global tour, refused to travel to Germany after Hitler came to power in 1933 and instead began conducting a summer medical practice in San Francisco, where his expertise in endocrinology eventually brought him into contact with Karl Bowman, and with Louise Lawrence and her friends. Benjamin's sympathy toward Lawrence and her circle, and his difference of opinion from that of his U.S.-trained colleagues in the 1949 case that marked the beginning of his career in transsexual medicine, was no doubt informed by the more progressive attitudes he had encountered at Hirschfeld's Institute for Sexual Science in Berlin.

Through her involvement at UCSF, Louise Lawrence met Virginia Prince. Born to a socially prominent family in Los Angeles in 1912, Prince had trained as a pharmacologist and was a postdoctoral researcher at UCSF when, while still living as a furtively cross-dressing man, she came in contact with Lawrence in 1942. That encounter quickly brought Prince into the orbit of the leading figures in transgender-oriented medical research. Schooled in transgender issues as part of that emerging network, Prince would eventually found the first enduring organizations in the United States devoted to transgender concerns. In spite of her open disdain for homosexuals, her frequently expressed negative opinion of transsexual surgeries, and her conservative stereotypes regarding masculinity and femininity, Prince (who began living full-time as a woman in 1968) has to be considered a central figure in the early history of the contemporary transgender political movement.

Virginia Prince returned to Los Angeles by the later 1940s, but she remained in touch with Lawrence and her network of transgender contacts, especially those living in Southern California, to whom Prince added her own growing circle of cross-dressing friends and acquaintances. In 1952, Prince and a group of transvestites who met regularly in Long Beach published an unprecedented newsletter—*Transvestia: The Journal of the American Society for Equality in Dress*—which they distributed to a mailing list consisting largely of Lawrence's correspondents. This little mimeographed publication, which existed for only two issues, is arguably the first overtly political transgender

transvestite

publication in U.S. history. Even its subtitle seems deliberately intended to evoke the dress reform activism of nineteenth-century first wave feminism. The periodical made a plea for the social toleration of transvestism, which it was careful to define as a practice of heterosexual men, distinct from homosexual drag.

Prince and her fledgling heterosexual transvestite rights movement soon had another identity category from which to distinguish themselves, once Christine Jorgensen burst onto the scene on December 1, 1952. Jorgensen, born male to Danish American parents in the Bronx in 1926, made international headlines with news of her successful genital transformation surgery in Copenhagen. A shy and somewhat effeminate youth, Jorgensen had been drafted into the army for a year after graduating high school, and she was pursuing a career as a photographer and film editor without any great success when she learned in 1949 that hormonal and surgical "sex change" was possible—in Europe. Given that the procedures she underwent in Copenhagen had been performed numerous times by then with little fanfare, her instant and worldwide celebrity came as something of a surprise (even though she herself, denials to the contrary, seems to have first called her story to the attention of the press). In a year when hydrogen bombs were being tested in the Pacific, war was raging in Korea, England crowned a new queen, and Jonas Salk invented the polio vaccine, Jorgensen was the most written-about topic in the media. Her story demonstrates yet again how historically contingent attention to transgender phenomena really is.

Part of the intense fascination with Jorgensen undoubtedly had to do with the fact that she was young, pretty, gracious, and dignified—but another part surely had to do with the mid-twentieth-century awe for scientific technology, which now could not only split atoms but also, apparently, turn a man into a woman. It had something to do with the fact that Jorgensen was the first transgender person to receive significant media attention who happened to be from the United States, which had risen to a new level of international geopolitical importance in the aftermath of World War II. The media made much of the fact that Jorgensen was an

plural
a soldier in the U.S. armed forces

© The Royal Library, Copenhagen

Christine Jorgensen became the most famous transgender person in the world when news of her 1952 "sex-change" surgery made headlines around the world.

"ex-GI," suggesting profound anxieties about masculinity and sexuality: There had been a great deal of attention to male homosexuality in the military during World War II, and maybe, some thought, gender transformation represented a solution to that perceived problem. But if a macho archetype such as "the soldier" could be transformed into a "blond bombshell," what did that mean for the average man? A final contributing factor was intense attention *after by war?* to social gender roles; (with millions of women who had worked outside the home during the war being steered back toward feminine domesticity, and millions of demobilized military men trying to fit themselves back into the civilian social order, questions of what made a man a man, or a woman a woman, and what their respective roles in life should be, were very much up for debate.) The feminist movement of the 1960s took shape in reaction to socially conservative solutions to these questions, and transgender issues have been a touchstone for those debates ever since fate thrust Christine Jorgensen into the spotlight.

Jorgensen, who went on to a successful career in show business, never considered herself a political activist, but she was well aware of the historic role she had to play as a public advocate for the issues that were central to her own life. Thousands of people wrote to her, many of them offering variations on the theme expressed by a French transgender woman who told Jorgensen that her story "touched me deeply and gave me a new hope for the future," or the person in upstate New York who wrote, "May God bless you for your courage so that other people may more clearly understand our problem." One correspondent told Jorgensen, "You are a champion of the downtrodden minorities who strive to live within their God-given rights"; another, in a letter to Jorgensen's parents, noted that there are "hundreds of thousands of people who look to Chris today as a sort of liberation." One man even suggested that Jorgensen function as a "central post office," much as Louise Lawrence had, through whom transgender people could get to know one another and share their problems, hopes, and fears. Jorgensen herself, after her return to the United States in 1953 generated an avalanche of attention from the paparazzi, told her doctors back in Copenhagen that she needed "as much good publicity as possible for the sake of all those to whom I am a representation of themselves."

Jorgensen's fame was a watershed event in transgender history. It brought an unprecedented level of public awareness to transgender issues, and it helped define the terms that would structure identity politics in the decades ahead. Christine Jorgensen was originally identified in the media as a "hermaphrodite," or intersex person, with a rare physical condition in which her "true" femaleness was masked by an only apparent maleness. But she was soon relabeled a "transvestite," in that older sense developed by Hirschfeld, in which the term referred to a wider range of transgender phenomena than it does today. That difference in usage is due largely to the efforts of Virginia Prince in the 1950s and '60s, partly in response to Jorgensen, to redefine transvestism as a synonym for heterosexual male cross-dressing. Harry Benjamin simultaneously started promoting the word "transsexual" to distinguish people such as Jorgensen, who sought surgical transformation, from people such as Prince, who did not.

Both transvestism and transsexuality came to be seen as something different from either homosexuality or intersexuality. All four categories strove to articulate the complex and variable interrelations between social gender, psychological identity, and physical sex—intellectual labor that informed the concept of a "sex/gender system" that became an important theoretical development within the emerging second wave feminist movement. Thus, by the end of the 1950s, the identity labels and border skirmishes between identity-based communities that still inform transgender activism today had fallen into place.

Government Harassment

In late 1959, a little event with big implications for transgender political history started to unfold in Los Angeles, when Virginia Prince pursued a friend's suggestion that she begin a personal correspondence with an individual on the East Coast; this third person, who self-represented as a lesbian, had expressed a desire through their mutual acquaintance to be put in written contact with Prince. Prince subsequently received a photograph from her East Coast correspondent (whom neither she nor her friend had ever met face to face), of two women being sexual with one another, which bore the caption "Me and You." Prince's correspondent invited her to "ask anything," and, as the intimacy of the correspondence deepened, Prince sent a letter describing a lesbian sexual fantasy involving the two of them. Prince's correspondent, it soon turned out, was another male cross-dresser, one who happened to be under surveillance by federal postal authorities for soliciting and receiving obscene materials, and whose personal mail was being examined surreptitiously by the government as part of an ongoing criminal investigation. In 1960, postal inspectors questioned Prince and ultimately decided, based on this incident, to prosecute her for the crime of distributing obscenity through the U.S. mail.

The events at the heart of this case—sort of an old-school, paper-based version of cybersex—prefigure some of the conundrums about identity that are now routine features of communication in the Internet age: How do you know if that person on MySpace really is, for example, an eighteen-year-old aspiring female pop vocalist from Portland rather than a balding forty-year-old accountant from Akron, when you have no way of knowing how the self-image that person presents online relates to the way he or she walks around in the world? What does "really" really mean, when you'll probably never meet face to face anyway? And why should the government care in the first place what two adults do in a private communication? Why should incongruence between various presentations of gender, or a frank but personal discussion of sexuality, be considered a matter of state concern or be considered obscene?

That such an incident became the target of a criminal investigation in the mid-twentieth century speaks volumes about the depth of transgender political struggles. What is at stake is not just what conventionally counts as political activity within modern society (such as staging protest rallies, passing laws, registering voters, or trying to change public opinion on an issue), but the very configurations of body, sense of self, practices of desire, modes of comportment, and forms of social relationships that qualify one in the first place as a fit subject for citizenship.

As the Prince prosecution demonstrates, the state's actions often regulate bodies, in ways both great and small, by enmeshing them within norms and expectations that determine what kinds of lives are deemed livable or useful and by shutting down the spaces of possibility and imaginative transformation where people's lives begin to exceed and escape the state's uses for them. This is a deep, structural problem within the logic of modern societies, which essentially perform a "cost-benefit" analysis when allocating social resources. People are expected to work in the ways demanded by the state—paying taxes, serving in the military, reproducing a population that will serve as the nation's future workforce, and performing socially useful services. Those who don't or can't function this way—whether through physical impairment, denial of opportunity, or personal choice—have a harder time sustaining themselves and justifying their very existence. Their situations—being black or female or disabled or queer—are not deemed to be valuable or worthy in their own right for the people who live those lives. Transgender lives are similarly devalued; they are neither considered useful or happy lives to live nor seen as offering any kind of value to society.

Such theoretical complexities notwithstanding, Prince's obscenity case, rooted as it was in government surveillance of the mail, helps situate early transgender political history within the anticommunist hysteria about national security at the height of the Cold War. It links particularly closely to the recurrent "pink scares" of the period, in which homosexuals were witch-hunted out of positions in government, industry, and education, based on the paranoid belief that such "perverts," besides being of dubious moral character, posed security risks because their illegal "lifestyle" made them vulnerable to blackmail or exploitation by enemies of the state. Consequently, the emerging transgender politics in the late 1950s and early '60s can't be cleanly separated from the history of official persecution of homosexuals. It needs to be understood as part of an overarching set of struggles about privacy, censorship, political dissent, minority rights, freedom of expression, and sexual liberation.

A 1954 survey of one hundred homosexual men in federal prisons noted, for example, that fifteen of them had been incarcerated directly as a result of their sexuality (the rest having been convicted of nonsexual crimes such as robbery or fraud), with nine of those fifteen convicted

Literature and Obscenity

Legal and social definitions of "obscenity" changed rapidly in the decades after World War II in ways that ultimately made information about variant gender and sexual practices (many of which were then deemed obscene) more easily accessible for many people. Cheap paperback books became very popular in this period, and—as long as the publishers could argue that the works had some literary, artistic, or historical significance—they often managed to evade censorship even when dealing with racy topics. Several transgender-themed mass market paperback books were published in the 1950s, most of them trying to cash in on the Christine Jorgensen craze. These included the 1953 intersex saga *Half*, by Jordan Park, and a reissue of the 1933 *Man into Woman*, Niels Hoyer's biography of the Danish painter Lille Elba, one of Hirschfeld's early transsexual patients.

Much of the so-called "homophile" nonfiction periodical literature from this period, which advocated social tolerance for homosexuals, was deemed obscene in the late 1950s and early 1960s. A notable obscenity case involved *ONE* magazine, published by the Los Angeles homophile organization ONE, starting in 1952; *ONE* has the distinction of being the first pro-gay publication to be sold openly at newsstands. In the mid-1950s, a federal district court in California declared it obscene and banned of sodomy and the other six committed for "postal law violations"—notably, as in Prince's case, for the use of the mail to send letters of solicitation to people with whom they sought sexual alliances. As the survey's author noted, "The violation in these cases stemmed from the fact that the letters were considered obscene."

Coincidentally or not—though probably not—between the time Prince wrote the "lesbian letter" that initially brought her to the attention of the authorities and the time she was charged with a serious crime, she had started publishing *Transvestia* magazine, which turned out to be the first long-running transgender-oriented periodical in the United States. Launched in 1960 and published several times a year into the 1980s, *Transvestia* revived the short-lived publication of the same name, described earlier, that Prince and her circle of cross-dressing friends had

it from the mail. That the U.S. Supreme Court subsequently overturned the decision in 1958 indicates how the legal climate on obscenity issues was beginning to shift, however—as does another landmark legal decision of this period. H. Lynn Womack, a former Georgetown University professor turned gay erotica publisher, successfully sued the postmaster general in 1961 for confiscating copies of his homoerotic *Grecian Guild* bodybuilder magazines. As late as 1964, though, Sanford Aday and Wallace de Ortega Maxey, two mail-order publishers of soft-core "sleaze paperbacks" (including transgender titles such as 1958's *The Lady Was a Man*), were convicted on federal charges of shipping "dirty books" across state lines, fined $25,000 each, and sentenced to a total of forty years in prison. The men were released a few years later, after the Supreme Court embraced a more lenient legal definition of obscenity. The gradual relaxation of obscenity standards reflected the broader cultural shifts of the "sexual revolution" fomented by Alfred Kinsey's best-selling reports on male and female sexuality (published in 1948 and 1953, respectively), the advent of *Playboy* magazine in 1953, the introduction of oral contraception ("the Pill") in 1960, and the more open-minded ethos of the youth counterculture that took shape among the post–World War II Baby Boom generation. The first long-running transgender community publications appeared just at this historical juncture, when new possibilities for publishing work on nonnormative gender and sexual expression were first starting to emerge.

published in 1952. Like the homophile literature it closely resembled, Prince's *Transvestia* excluded explicit sexual content and focused on social commentary, educational outreach, self-help advice, and autobiographical vignettes drawn from her own life and the lives of her readers. The magazine significantly shifted the political meaning of transvestism, moving it away from being the expression of a criminalized sexual activity and toward being the common denominator of a new (and potentially political) identity-based minority community. That shift undoubtedly fueled the determination of federal prosecutors to convict Prince of a felony and to halt the distribution of *Transvestia*, just as they had tried to halt the distribution of *ONE* and other homophile publications.

In such a volatile legal landscape, things could have turned out much worse than they did when Virginia Prince's case went to trial in Los Angeles Federal Court in February 1961. She pleaded guilty to a lesser charge and avoided serving time in prison by accepting five years' probation, during which time she agreed to refrain from public cross-dressing and from using the mail for indecent purposes. Although postal authorities tried to ban distribution of *Transvestia*, the court, reflecting the trend toward increasingly lenient definitions of obscenity, did not find it to be obscene, and postal inspectors never pursued charges against the publication's subscribers. In 1962, with the tacit consent of high-level U.S. Postal Service bureaucrats with whom Prince had been pleading her case, the federal judge declared Prince's probationary sentence to have been fulfilled; she never thereafter had another brush with the law.

The First Modern Transgender Organizations

While her obscenity case was working its way through court, Virginia Prince founded the first long-lasting transgender organizations in the United States. In 1961, she convened a clandestine meeting in Los Angeles of several local *Transvestia* subscribers—instructing them all, unbeknownst to one another, to rendezvous at a certain hotel room, each carrying a pair of stockings and high heels concealed in a brown paper bag. Once the men were assembled, Prince instructed them all to put on the shoes she had asked them to bring—simultaneously implicating all of them in the stigmatized activity of cross-dressing and thereby forming a communal (and self-protective) bond. This group became known as the Hose and Heels Club and began meeting regularly. In 1962, once Prince's legal troubles were safely behind her, her community-organizing efforts kicked into high gear. She transformed the Hose and Heels Club into the "Alpha Chapter" of a new national organization, the Foundation for Personality Expression (FPE), which she modeled on the collegiate sorority system and which soon had several chapters across the country.

Prince used FPE, later known as the Society for the Second Self, or Tri-Ess, as a platform to promote her personal philosophy about gender, which she outlined in books such as *How to Be a Woman Though Male* and *The Transvestite and His Wife*. Prince believed that cross-dressing allowed men to express their "full personality" in a world that required a strict division between the masculine and the feminine. FPE meetings, which were highly secretive affairs held in private homes or hotel rooms, tended to involve the conduct of organizational business, a presentation by an invited speaker, and time for socializing. Prince personally controlled membership in these groups well into the 1970s, and she limited members to married heterosexual men, excluding gays, male-to-female transsexuals, and biologically female individuals.

The membership restrictions of FPE, and the form and content of its meetings, demonstrate a familiar pattern in minority identity politics in U.S. history—it is often the most privileged elements of a population affected by a particular civil injustice or social oppression who have the opportunity to organize first. In organizing around the one thing that interferes with or complicates their privilege, their organizations tend to reproduce that very privilege. This was certainly true of FPE, which was explicitly geared toward protecting the privileges of predominantly white, middle-class men who used their money and access to private property to create a space in which they could express a stigmatized aspect of themselves in a way that didn't jeopardize their jobs or social standing. Prince herself took the leading role in driving wedges between

Drag Balls

While white suburban transgender people were sneaking out to clandestine meetings, many transgender people of color were highly visible parts of urban culture. "Miss Major" came out as trans as a teenager in the late 1950s in Chicago. In this 1998 interview, she describes the African American drag ball subculture of her youth.

We had the balls then, where we could go out and dress up. You had to keep your eyes open, had to watch your back, but you learned how to deal with that, and how to relax into it, and how to have a good time. It was a pleasure, a wonder—even with the confusion. We didn't know at the time that we were questioning our gender. We just knew that this felt right. There wasn't all this terminology, all this labeling—you know what I mean?

[The balls] were phenomenal! It was like going to the Oscars show today. Everybody dressed up. Guys in tuxedos, queens in gowns that you would not believe—I mean, things that they would have been working on all year. There was a queen in the South Side who would do the South City Ball. There was one on the North Side who would do the Maypole Ball. There were different ones in different areas at different times. And the straight people who would come and watch, they were different than the ones who come today. They just appreciated what was going on. They would applaud the girls when they were getting out of one Cadillac after another. It was just that the money was there, and the timing was right, and the energy was there to do this thing with an intensity that people just don't seem to have today. It seems to have dissipated. Then it was always a wonder—whether you participated, whether you watched, whether you just wore a little cocktail dress and a small fur coat—it was just a nice time.

Four "queens" arrive at a San Francisco drag ball in 1965.

© Henri Lelen Collection

transvestite, transsexual, gay and lesbian, and feminist communities, and she did not envision an inclusive, expansive, progressive, and multifaceted transgender movement. And yet, she undoubtedly played a key role in founding just such a movement. After beginning to live full-time as a woman in 1968, Prince worked vigorously for many years to promote various transgender causes (such as the ability to change the gender designation on state-issued identification documents). Her legal troubles in the early 1960s were potentially quite serious, and if for nothing else, she should be honored in transgender political history for the personal courage she showed in facing a felony conviction and federal prison sentence, all for the ostensible crime of "using the mail while transgendered."

CHAPTER 3

TRANSGENDER LIBERATION

As TRANSGENDER PHENOMENA CAME UNDER mounting social and medical
regulation in the United States between the 1850s and the 1950s, daily
life for some transgender people shifted into increasingly distinct public
and private spheres. Class and race privilege encouraged white people
with transgender feelings, especially if they enjoyed a measure of social
respectability or financial security, to construct their identities in isolation,
to engage in cross-dressing only furtively, and to form networks with
others like themselves only at great risk, unless they were willing to present
themselves as people in need of medical or psychiatric help. Ironically,
it was the most closeted and least political segment of the transgender
population that first formed sustainable organizations and first became
targets of federal prosecution. At roughly the same time as Virginia Prince's
run-in with the postal inspectors, however, another form of transgender
political history began to take shape among people who lacked many of
the privileges enjoyed by members of Prince's Foundation for Personality
Expression. These transgender people had a very different relationship to
(or membership in) gay communities and communities of color, as well as
to public space and to the police. They confronted on a daily basis all the
things that FPE's membership worked so hard to avoid.

Militant Foreshadowings

In a 2005 interview, John Rechy, author of *City of Night* and other classic
mid-twentieth-century novels set in the gritty urban underworlds where
sexual outlaws and gender nonconformists carved out spaces they could call

Street Queens

John Rechy, born in 1934 in El Paso, Texas, is the author of more than a dozen books, many of which revolve around his youthful involvement in the world of male hustlers. *City of Night*, excerpted below, paints a vivid portrait of "Miss Destiny" and other "street queens" in Los Angeles in the early 1960s.

As I stand on the corner of 6th and Main, a girlish Negro Youngman with round eyes swishes up: "Honey," she says—just like that and shrilly loudly, enormous gestures punctuating her words, "you look like you jest got into town. If you aint gotta place, I got a real nice pad...." I only stare at her. "Why, baby," she says, "dont you look so startled—this is L.A.!—and thank God for that! Even queens like me got certain rights! ... Well," she sighs, "I guess you wanna look around first. So I'll jest give you my number." She handed me a card, with her name, telephone number, address: Elaborately Engraved. "Jest you call me—anytime!" she said....

Looking at Chuck and Miss Destiny—as she rushes on now about the Turbulent Times—I know the scene: Chuck the masculine cowboy and Miss Destiny the femme queen: making it from day to park to bar to day like all the others in that ratty world of downtown L.A. which I will make my own: the world of queens technically men but no one thinks of them that way—always "she"—their "husbands" being the masculine

their own, spoke of a previously undocumented incident in May of 1959, when transgender and gay resentment of police oppression erupted into collective resistance. According to Rechy, it happened at Cooper's Donuts, a coffeehouse that stayed open all night on a rough stretch of Main Street in Los Angeles, which happened to be situated between two popular gay bars. An ethnically mixed crowd of drag queens and male hustlers, many of them Latino or African American, frequented Cooper's, along with the people who enjoyed their company or bought their sexual services. Police cars regularly patrolled the vicinity and often stopped to question people in the area for no reason at all. The police would demand identification—

vagrants—fleetingly and often out of convenience sharing the queens' pads—never considering theyre involved with another man (the queen), and only for scoring (which is making or taking sexmoney, getting a meal, making a pad)—he is himself not considered "queer"—he remains, in the vocabulary of that world, "trade."

It was real-life people such as Rechy's character Miss Destiny who, in the 1960s, were among the first gender-variant people to become militant at places such as Cooper's. However, claiming figures such as Miss Destiny as part of transgender history is controversial in some quarters, because some people say that the word "transgender" didn't exist back then, or that some queens considered themselves gay men rather than transwomen. But some queens from this period did move on to live their lives as women, and they do look back on their experiences as being part of transgender history—and many contemporary trans people certainly find inspiration in the fierce determination exhibited by people decades ago who lived lives in public that challenged conventional expectations for what it meant to be a man or a woman, whatever those people thought of themselves.

For a good history of male hustler culture, including the involvement of transwomen, see Mack Friedman's *Strapped for Cash: A History of American Hustler Culture*, published in 2003. Hubert Selby Jr. delivers an emotionally devastating portrait of working-class queer sexuality in post–World War II America in his *Last Exit to Brooklyn* (first published in 1964), which integrates the story of a transgender character, Georgette, into the overarching story of life in a gritty urban neighborhood.

which, for transgender people whose appearance might not match the name or gender designation on their IDs, often led to arrest on suspicion of prostitution, vagrancy, loitering, or many other so-called "nuisance crimes." On that night in May 1959, when the police came in and arbitrarily started rounding up the drag queen patrons of Cooper's Donuts, the rest of the customers decided to resist en masse. The incident started with customers throwing doughnuts at the cops and ended with fighting in the streets, as squad cars and paddy wagons converged on the scene to make arrests. In the ensuing chaos, many people who had been arrested, including Rechy, escaped into the night.

The disturbance at Cooper's seems to have been a spontaneous outburst of frustration, with no lasting consequences, and it was no doubt typical of other unrecorded and previously unremembered acts of spur-of-the-moment resistance to antitransgender and antigay oppression. A similar, though nonviolent, incident took place in Philadelphia in 1965 at Dewey's, a lunch counter and late-night coffeehouse much like Cooper's, which had been popular since the 1940s with gays, lesbians, drag queens, and street prostitutes as a place to go after the bars had closed. In April of 1965, Dewey's started refusing to serve young customers who wore what one gay newspaper of the day euphemistically described as "nonconformist clothing," claiming that "gay kids" were driving away other business. Customers rallied to protest, and on April 25, more than 150 patrons were turned away by the management. Three teenagers (two male and one female) refused to leave after being denied service in what appears to be the first act of civil disobedience over antitransgender discrimination; they, along with a gay activist who advised them of their legal rights, were arrested (and subsequently found guilty on misdemeanor charges of disorderly conduct). During the next week, Dewey's patrons and members of Philadelphia's homosexual community set up an informational picket line at the restaurant, where they passed out thousands of pieces of literature protesting the lunch counter's treatment of gender-variant young people. On May 2, activists staged another sit-in. The police were again called in but this time made no arrests; the restaurant's management backed down and promised "an immediate cessation of all indiscriminate denials of service." *(great*

The Dewey's incident, like the one at Cooper's, demonstrates the overlap between gay and transgender activism in the working-class districts of major U.S. cities in spite of tensions and prejudices within both groups. Historian Marc Stein, in *City of Sisterly and Brotherly Loves: Lesbian and Gay Philadelphia, 1945–1972*, tells how the Janus Society, Philadelphia's main gay and lesbian organization at the time, issued the following statement in its newsletter after the events of May 2, 1965:

All too often, there is a tendency to be concerned with the rights of homosexuals as long as they somehow appear to be heterosexual, whatever that is. The masculine woman and the feminine man often are looked down upon . . . but the Janus Society is concerned with the worth of an individual and the manner in which she or he comports himself. What is offensive today we have seen become the style of tomorrow, and even if what is offensive today remains offensive tomorrow to some persons, there is no reason to penalize non-conformist behavior unless there is direct anti-social behavior connected with it.

The Dewey's incident further illustrates the extent to which the tactics of minority rights activism cross-fertilized different movements. Lunch counter sit-ins had been developed as a form of protest to oppose racial segregation in the South, but they proved equally effective when used to promote the interests of sexual and gender minorities. It would be a mistake, however, to think that the African American civil rights struggle simply "influenced" early gay and transgender activism at Dewey's, for to do so would be to assume that all the gay and transgender people involved were white. Many of the queer people who patronized Dewey's were themselves people of color, and they were not "borrowing" a tactic developed by another movement.

The Compton's Cafeteria Riot of 1966

By the middle of the 1960s, life in the United States was being transformed by several large-scale social movements. The post–World War II Baby Boom generation was coming into young adulthood at the very moment the U.S. war in Vietnam was beginning to escalate. A youth-oriented cultural rebellion began to unfold, in which countercultural styles in music and fashion—rock music, psychedelic drugs, mod clothing, free love—offered significant challenges to an older generation's notion of acceptable gender and sexual expression. Long hair on men, and button-fly blue jeans on women, actually made political statements about the war, the military draft, and the general drift of mainstream society. The African American civil rights movement was reaching a crescendo, buoyed by passage in 1964 of the Civil Rights Act and other milestone legislation, as well as by the birth of a radical new Black Power movement. Similar ethnic pride and liberation movements were beginning to vitalize Chicano and Native American people. To a certain extent, the simultaneous white gay liberation and radical feminist movements modeled themselves on these ethnic movements, conceptualizing homosexual people and women as oppressed social minority groups. National political life, which had been thrown into turmoil after the 1963 assassination of President John F. Kennedy, reached a tragic low point with the 1968 assassinations of his brother Robert F. Kennedy and the Reverend Martin Luther King Jr. The most militant phase of the transgender movement for social change, from 1966 to 1969, was part of this massive social upheaval.

The 1966 Compton's Cafeteria Riot in San Francisco's seedy Tenderloin neighborhood was similar to earlier incidents at Cooper's and Dewey's; for the first time, however, direct action in the streets by transgender people resulted in lasting institutional change. One weekend night in August—the precise date is unknown—Compton's, a twenty-four-hour cafeteria at the corner of Turk and Taylor streets, was buzzing with its usual late-night crowd of drag queens, hustlers, slummers, cruisers, runaway teens, and down-and-out neighborhood regulars. The restaurant's management became annoyed by a noisy young crowd of queens at one table who seemed be spending a lot of time without spending a lot of money, and it called in the police to roust them—as it had been doing with increasing frequency throughout the summer. A surly police officer, accustomed to manhandling Compton's clientele with impunity, grabbed the arm of one of the queens and tried to drag her away. She unexpectedly threw her coffee in his face, however, and a melee erupted: Plates, trays, cups, and silverware flew through the air at the startled police officers, who ran outside and called for backup. Compton's customers turned over the tables and smashed the plate-glass windows and then poured out of the restaurant and into the streets. The paddy wagons arrived, and street fighting broke out in Compton's vicinity, all around the corner of Turk and Taylor. Drag queens beat the police with their heavy purses and kicked them with their

Compton's Cafeteria in San Francisco's Tenderloin neighborhood was the scene of an early episode of transgender resistance to social oppression when transgender women, gay men, and prostitutes fought back against police harassment there in August 1966.

high-heeled shoes. A police car was vandalized, a newspaper stand was burned to the ground, and—in the words of the best available source on what happened that night, a retrospective account by gay liberation activist Reverend Raymond Broshears, published in the program of San Francisco's first Gay Pride march in 1972—"general havoc was raised in the Tenderloin." The small restaurant had been packed when the fighting broke out, so the riot probably involved fifty or sixty patrons, plus police officers and any neighborhood residents or late-night passersby who jumped into the fray.

Contextualizing Compton's

Although the exact date of the riot remains a mystery—none of the mainstream San Francisco daily newspapers covered the story; police reports have conveniently disappeared; surviving participants who were interviewed decades later remembered only that it happened on a summer weekend night; and Broshears's account (written six years after the fact) said only that the riot took place in August—its underlying causes are reasonably clear. Understanding why the riot happened where and when it did reveals a great deal about the issues that have historically motivated the transgender social justice struggle and helps us understand similar dynamics at work today.

The location of the riot was by no means random. San Francisco's downtown Tenderloin neighborhood had been a sex-work district since the early 1900s. In fact, if you look up the word "tenderloin" in many dictionaries, you'll find that one slang meaning is actually an inner-city vice district controlled by corrupt police officers. As large cities formed in the United States in the nineteenth century, they typically developed certain neighborhoods in which activities that weren't tolerated elsewhere—prostitution, gambling, drug taking, and sexually explicit entertainment—were effectively permitted. Police usually turned a blind eye to this illicit activity—often because the cops on the beat, and sometimes their superiors in the station house, were getting a cut of the profits in exchange for not arresting the individuals engaged in the criminalized activities. Only occasionally, when civic or religious groups mounted a morality crusade or some sex scandal implicated a high-ranking politician, did police make "sweeps" of the neighborhood. Soon enough, however, it would be business as usual again.

The Tenderloin was just this sort of neighborhood. Much of the so-called vice trade in the neighborhood was supported by nonresidents of one sort or another—downtown office workers getting a "massage" on their lunch breaks, barhoppers looking for a place to sober up after last call, teenage thrill seekers and out-of-town tourists eager for some racy big-city entertainment, suburban junkies looking to score. But the neighborhood's resident population tended to be those who could least afford to live elsewhere, or who were prevented from doing so: released convicts and parolees, old-timers on small pensions, recent immigrants, pimps, prostitutes, drug addicts, alcoholics—and transgender women.

Housing and employment discrimination against transgender people are still legal in most places in the United States, and this discrimination was even more common in the past than it is now. In the 1960s, more so than today, a person who looked transgendered would be less likely to be rented to and would have a great deal of trouble finding work. As a result, a great many transgender women lived in the Tenderloin in cheap residential hotels, many of them along Turk Street near Compton's. To meet their basic survival needs they often worked as prostitutes or as maids in the hotels and bars where their friends sold sex. While most people who participated in the Tenderloin's illicit economy of sex, drugs, and after-hours entertainment were free to come and go, the neighborhood functioned as more of an involuntary containment zone for transgender women. Police actually helped concentrate a population of transgender women in the Tenderloin by directing them to go there when they were picked up in other parts of the city.

The police could be especially vicious to "street queens," whom they considered bottom-of-the-barrel sex workers, and who were the least able to complain about mistreatment. Transgender women working the streets were often arrested on suspicion of prostitution even if they were just going to the corner store or talking with friends; they might be driven around in squad cars for hours, forced to perform oral sex, strip-searched, or, after arriving at the jail, humiliated in front of other prisoners. Transgender women in jail often would have their heads forcibly shaved, or if they resisted, be placed in solitary confinement in "the hole." And because they were legally men (with male genitalia in spite of their social lives as women, and often in spite of having breasts and no facial hair) they would be placed in the men's jail, where their femininity made them especially vulnerable to sexual assault, rape, and murder.

This chronically bad situation became even worse in the mid-1960s, when U.S. involvement in the war in Vietnam escalated. Wartime is typically a time of heightened surveillance of commercial sexual activity in cities where large numbers of troops are being mobilized for deployment. Military and civilian police, along with public health officials, cooperate to prevent troops (many of them quite eager to escape thoughts of battlefield death with wild sexual escapades) from acquiring sexually transmitted infections that might compromise their combat readiness, and which might even be spread within the ranks by homosexual activity. There were wartime crackdowns on prostitution in San Francisco during the Spanish-American War in the Philippines in the 1890s, during World War II in the 1940s, and during the Korean conflict in the 1950s. Among the hardest-hit establishments in San Francisco during the crackdown associated with the 1964–66 escalation of U.S. troops in Vietnam were the gay and drag bars, which even then catered to the "Don't ask, don't tell" military crowd.

Yet another factor that changed an already grim situation from bad to worse for transgender women in the Tenderloin was the effect of urban renewal and redevelopment. Their increasingly serious plight was directly related to very broad-scale social and economic changes. As in other major U.S. cities, San Francisco's built environment underwent a major transformation in the two decades after World War II as the city "modernized." Some of this redevelopment was driven by needs created during the war years. Many working-class and poor people had left small towns for war-related work in the major coastal cities in the 1940s and had been housed temporarily in quickly constructed housing projects. When the war was over, many soldiers came home from overseas to find their families living in new cities rather than their old hometowns, putting a further burden on city housing. Complicating things even further, many of these new urban residents were people of color, who were not well integrated or welcomed into the fabric of white-dominated cities once the need for their wartime labor had passed. Part of the government's response to the problems of postwar adjustment was to fund big new housing projects for working-class people and to help former soldiers buy suburban homes with low-interest home loans.

San Francisco business elites and city planners, like their counterparts elsewhere, tried to turn the necessity of solving pressing urban problems into an opportunity to reenvision the city in ways that reflected their own interests. They imagined a new and improved San Francisco Bay Area, with San Francisco itself functioning as the center of finance, culture, high-tech industry, and tourism for the entire region. Surrounding San Francisco to the east and south would be a semicircle of heavy industry, and beyond that, residential suburbs. New freeways and public transportation systems would have to be built to bring office workers from the suburbs to the center of business downtown.

In the process of reorganizing the entire fabric of daily life, old neighborhoods had to be destroyed or relocated. To one side of the Tenderloin were the Fillmore and Western Addition neighborhoods that had become mostly black during the war years; residents there were forcibly removed to new housing projects on the edge of the city, in Bayview and Hunters Point, and entire blocks bulldozed for newer high-density apartments. To the other side of the Tenderloin was the South of Market neighborhood (sometimes called Skid Row), which had revolved around the maritime economy—lots of short-term residential hotels and rooming for sailors who would stay in town for only a few months, working-class bars and restaurants, and industries related to shipping and commerce. During post–World War II redevelopment, San Francisco's port was shut down and moved across the bay to Oakland; doing so required breaking the waterfront labor unions, which created less favorable economic conditions for many working-class people. The waterfront-oriented district itself started to become derelict and was then condemned and slated for redevelopment as museums, convention facilities, and other tourist-oriented establishments. The physical destruction of these important black and working-class neighborhoods in the 1960s left the Tenderloin as the last remaining enclave of affordable housing in downtown San Francisco. New residents coming in from adjacent areas began to displace the Tenderloin's most vulnerable and at-risk residents—transgender women who worked as street prostitutes and lived in the cheapest hotels.

In response to the massive social dislocations of urban renewal and redevelopment, Tenderloin residents launched a grassroots campaign for economic justice in 1965. They were inspired in equal measures by the socially progressive gospel preached by the Reverend Martin Luther King Jr. and other ministers in the civil rights struggle, by the federal government's new War on Poverty programs, and by the vision of radically participatory democratic social movements outlined by Saul Alinsky in his activist handbook *Reveille for Radicals*. Neighborhood activists, including many members of San Francisco's homophile organizations and street-outreach ministers from Glide Memorial

United Methodist Church, went door to door in the Tenderloin, organizing the neighborhood and mobilizing it for social change. Their immediate goal was to establish needed social services by qualifying the neighborhood for federal antipoverty funding. Through a quirk of circumstances, the Tenderloin, one of the poorest areas of the city, was initially excluded from plans to direct more federal funding toward eradicating poverty in San Francisco because of the fact that its residents in the 1960s were almost all white. The coalition of grassroots groups that oversaw the local distribution of federal grant money was based in the black neighborhoods of Bayview, Hunters Point, the Fillmore, and the Western Addition, in the predominantly Latino Mission District, and in Chinatown. The Tenderloin organizers not only had to document economic need in their neighborhood; they also had to persuade poor communities of color that adding an additional antipoverty target zone predominately populated by white people would be the right thing to do, even if that meant the already existing zones got a smaller slice of a fixed amount of money. Compounding matters even further, most of the white people were queer, and most of the people of color were straight. The eventual establishment of the Central City Anti-Poverty Program thus represented a singular accomplishment in the history of U.S. progressive politics: the first successful multiracial gay/straight alliance for economic justice.

Tenderloin activists involved in the antipoverty organizing campaign were striving to create conditions in which people could truly participate in structuring the society they lived in instead of just reacting to changes created by others. One unexpected consequence of neighborhood mobilization was the formation of Vanguard, an organization made up mostly of young gay hustlers and transgender people. Vanguard, which formed in the summer of 1966, is the earliest known queer youth organization in the United States. Its name, which signaled members' perception that they were the cutting edge of a new social movement, shows how seriously they took the ideals of radical democracy. The group's leader even took a nom de guerre, Jean-Paul Marat, after a famous figure in the French Revolution.

Social Justice Ministry

Glide Memorial United Methodist Church in San Francisco's Tenderloin has been a hotbed of progressive social activism since the early 1960s. It was founded in 1929 by Lilly Glide, the daughter of a prominent family of philanthropists in San Francisco, as a "working man's mission," a place where down-and-out folks could go for a bowl of soup in exchange for listening to a sermon. The congregation had dwindled by the late 1950s, but the church still had a large endowment from the Glide family, prompting the national Methodist leadership to transform Glide Memorial into a model for a new kind of urban Christian ministry, of the sort inspired by the Reverend Martin Luther King Jr.'s civil rights activism. Under the leadership of the Reverend Cecil Williams, who became head pastor in 1966, Glide has become one of the most famous liberal Christian churches in America, supported by the likes of Maya Angelou, Oprah Winfrey, and Bill Clinton. The 2006 Will Smith film *Pursuit of Happyness* recounts the story of formerly homeless single parent Chris Gardner, whose ultimate rise to fortune and fame was made possible by the support he received from Glide during the most difficult period of his life.

One of the most daring social initiatives launched by Glide in the early 1960s was to establish the Council on Religion and the Homosexual (CRH), the first ecumenical organization to bring the problem of antigay discrimination to the attention of the liberal Protestant churches. Activist ministers at Glide worked with leaders of the early homophile, or gay rights, organizations, to shift the focus of religious concern away from condemning the supposed sin of homosexuality toward administering to the daily needs of people who suffered—through the loss of family, friends, work, or sense of emotional well-being—because of their sexual orientation. A police raid on a 1965 drag masquerade ball, a fund-raiser for the CRH, is widely credited with putting gay rights on the agenda of straight civil rights activists.

Glide Memorial also played an important role in transgender history. Activist ministers there helped organize Vanguard in 1966, an organization for gay and transgender street kids who lived in the Tenderloin; Conversion Our Goal, the first transsexual peer support group in the United States, held its meetings at Glide starting in 1967, and it published its newsletter there. Through the years, Glide has remained a powerful voice speaking out on issues that affect marginalized communities. As a result of Glide's commitment to work on behalf of all the residents of its neighborhood, attending to the needs of transgender people has been integrated into a broader vision of social justice.

Vanguard described itself as "an organization of, by, and for the kids on the streets." Its goals were to promote a sense of self-worth among its members, to offer mutual support and companionship, to bring youth issues to the attention of older people, and to assert its presence in the neighborhood. One of the group's early flyers urged people to think past racial divisions and focus instead on shared living conditions: "You've heard about Black Power and White Power," the flyer said, before telling its readers to "get ready for Street Power." The Vanguard members' basic approach was to treat the street as their home: They cleaned it up, challenged people coming into the neighborhood for the sex and drugs trade to pick up their dirty needles and empty bottles, and intervened with people acting in inappropriate ways. Vanguard's first major political action, however, was to confront the management of Compton's Cafeteria over its poor treatment of transgender women. Compton's Cafeteria functioned as a chill-out lounge for the whole neighborhood; for young people who often had no homes, families, or legal employment, who were marginalized by their gender or sexuality, it provided an especially vital resource.

Vanguard held its meetings at Compton's, and during the course of the summer of 1966, tensions there had been on the rise. As the restaurant's customers increasingly claimed its turf as their own, the management asserted its property rights and business interests more and more strongly. It instituted a "service charge" for each customer to make up for income lost to tables of young people "camping out" and not buying any food, but

Vanguard, founded in July 1966, was the first gay and transgender youth organization in the United States. The members published a psychedelically illustrated magazine (also called Vanguard) from the mid-1960s until the early 1970s.

© Vanguard magazine

it applied the charge in a discriminatory manner. It hired security guards to harass the street kids and shoo them outside, particularly the transgender youth. And with greater and greater frequency, it called the cops. In July, Vanguard worked with ministers from Glide and with older members of San Francisco's homophile organizations to set up a picket line protesting the mistreatment of its members, much as the customers and gay activists in Philadelphia had done at Dewey's. In San Francisco, however, the restaurant's management turned a deaf ear to the complaints. Soon after the picket failed to produce any results, frustration boiled over into militant resistance.

One thing that made the incident at Compton's different from similar incidents at Cooper's and Dewey's was a new attitude toward transgender healthcare in the United States. Doctors in Europe had been using hormones and surgery for more than fifty years to improve the quality of life for transgender people who desired those procedures; doctors in the United States had always been reluctant to do so, however, fearing that to operate or administer hormones would only be colluding with a deranged person's fantasy of "changing sex" or would be enabling a homosexual person to engage in perverse sexual practices. And after 1949, California Attorney General Pat Brown's legal opinion against genital modification created legal exposure for doctors who performed genital surgery. This situation began to change in July of 1966, just before the Compton's Cafeteria riot, when Dr. Harry Benjamin published a pathbreaking book, *The Transsexual Phenomenon*. In it, he used the research he had conducted with transgender patients during the past seventeen years to advocate for the same style of treatment that Magnus Hirschfeld had promoted in Germany before the Nazi takeover. Benjamin essentially argued that a person's gender identity could not be changed, and that the doctor's responsibility was thus to help transgender people live fuller and happier lives in the gender they identified as their own. Benjamin's book helped bring about a sea change in medical and legal attitudes. Within a few months of its publication, the first "sex change" program in the United States was established at the Johns Hopkins University Medical School.

The sudden availability of a new medical paradigm for addressing transgender needs undoubtedly played a role in creating a flash point at Compton's, where long-standing grievances finally erupted into violence. When people struggling against an injustice have no hope that anything will ever change, they use their strength to survive; when they think that their actions matter, that same strength becomes a force for positive change. Because Benjamin worked in San Francisco for part of every year, some of his patients were the very Tenderloin street queens who would soon start fighting back to improve their lives. They were intimately familiar with his work. Of course, not every male-bodied person who lived and worked in women's clothes in the Tenderloin wanted surgery or hormones, and not all of them thought of themselves as women or as transsexuals. But many of them did. And for those who did, the changes in medical-service provision that Benjamin recommended must have been an electrifying call to action. The next time the police raided their favorite neighborhood hangout, they had something to stand up for.

Looking back, it's easy to see how the Compton's Cafeteria riot in 1966 was related to very large-scale political, social, and economic developments and was not just an isolated little incident unrelated to other things that were going on in the world. The circumstances that created the conditions for the riot in the first place continue to be relevant in the transgender movement today: discriminatory policing practices in minority communities, harmful urban land-use policies, the unsettling domestic consequences of U.S. foreign wars, access to healthcare, civil rights activism aiming to expand individual liberties and social tolerance on matters of sexuality and gender, and political coalition building around the structural injustices that affect many different communities. The violent resistance to the oppression of transgender people at Compton's Cafeteria did not solve the problems that transgender people in the Tenderloin faced daily. It did, however, create a space in which it became possible for the city of San Francisco to begin relating differently to its transgender citizens—to begin treating them, in fact, as citizens with legitimate needs instead of simply as a problem to get rid of. That shift in awareness was a crucial step for the contemporary transgender social justice movement—the beginning of a new relationship to state power and social legitimacy. It would not have happened the way that it did without direct action in the streets on the part of transgender women who were fighting for their own survival.

A New Network of Services and Organizations

Several important developments for the transgender movement took place in San Francisco in the months after the Compton's Cafeteria riot. The Central City Anti-Poverty Program Office opened that fall as a result of the Tenderloin neighborhood organizing campaign. This multiservice agency included an office for the police community-relations liaison officer to the homophile community, a police sergeant by the name of Elliott Blackstone. One afternoon shortly after the agency opened, a transgender neighborhood resident named Louise Ergestrasse came into Blackstone's office, threw a copy of Benjamin's *The Transsexual Phenomenon* on his desk, and demanded that Blackstone do something for "her people." Blackstone was willing to be educated on the matter, and he soon took a leading role in changing police treatment of transgender people. Another group of transgender Tenderloin activists, led by MTF transsexual Wendy Kohler, a patient of Benjamin's, started working with activist doctor Joel Fort at a unit of the San Francisco Public Health Department called the Center for Special Problems. A few months later, in early 1967, a group of transgender people began meeting at Glide Memorial in the Tenderloin, where they formed Conversion Our Goal, or COG, the first known transsexual peer support group in the United States.

Between 1966 and 1968, these groups and individuals formed an interlocking network of transgender activists, allies, and services. COG, which published the short-lived *COG Newsletter*, provided an initial point of contact for transgender people seeking medical services, who were then steered toward the Center for Special Problems, which offered additional group support sessions, psychological counseling, hormone prescriptions, and, eventually, when a "sex change" clinic was established at nearby Stanford University Medical School, surgery referrals. Perhaps most important, however, the center provided ID cards for transgender patients that matched their social genders. It was a simple laminated piece of orange paper, signed by a public health doctor, bearing the name actually used by the patient, the patient's address, and the statement: "[Patient's name] is under treatment for transsexualism at the Center for Special Problems." While the ID card did "out" those carrying it as transsexual, it nevertheless allowed people to open bank accounts and do other things that required identification. Without that card, transsexuals living in a social gender other than the one assigned to them at birth were essentially "undocumented workers" who had great difficulty finding legal employment.

Meanwhile, the Central City Anti-Poverty Program offered transgender women in the Tenderloin the opportunity to leave prostitution, teaching them clerical skills through the Neighborhood Youth Corps training programs. Elliott Blackstone worked to dissuade his colleagues in the police department from arresting transgender people simply for using the "wrong" toilets or cross-dressing in public, and he promoted many other progressive attitudes toward transgender issues. Significantly, a California State Supreme Court ruling in 1962 had struck down laws that criminalized cross-dressing, but the practice of arresting cross-dressed individuals nevertheless persisted. Police attitudes, as well as laws, needed to change, and Blackstone played a vital role in challenging police practices at the practical level.

Although most of the city-funded aspects of the San Francisco–based transgender support network that developed in the mid-1960s continue to operate even now, the community-based organizations proved ephemeral, as such groups often are. COG split into two competing factions within a year of its founding. The major faction regrouped as the equally short-lived National Sexual-Gender Identification Council (NSGIC) under the leadership of Wendy Kohler, whose main accomplishment was holding a one-day conference at Glide Church on transsexual issues. The minor faction, which

TENDERLOIN TRANSEXUAL

Dear Vanguard:
I am a resident of a Tenderloin hotel. I live constantly in the clothes of a woman although I an a biological male. In this letter to you, I want to give moral support to anyone who may want to do what I've done, but isn't sure of quite how.

The change in me came after years of living without an identity. Not long ago I didn't know who I was. Now I know.

In New York I worked as an actor. I was in search of an identity then and theater allowed me to pose at least as a playwright's character. Unfortunately, I couldn't be on the stage 24 hours a day. The majority of my life was spent trying to play a role that I didn't fit. Though I was born with a male appendage, I couldn't consider myself a male. My psychiatrists and psychologists considered me sane, and normal in every way but for my anti-social yearning. My great trouble was inside. Biologically a male and psychologically a female. My doctors told me that it's not easy for someone born with the "wrong" physical attributes for the inside of him.

knew I was very alone.

However I was not without hope. I am now a woman with a few abnormalities which can be corrected surgically. I believe this. In my soul I know that it's true.

So, I left New York and came to San Francisco. I left the stage agony and I became aware that it was necessary for me to evolve above it. My objective was clear- adjustment to what I really was and finding out where I really was.

I began working at a T.L. hotel to earn enough money for living expenses and to cover the cost of electro lysis and hormone treatments. Until I accepted the job, there, "queen hotels" and living-in-drag were unknown to me. A well-known TL personality had to tell me all there was to know. Gradually through my own efforts I pulled through temptation and frustration. It certainly was easier for me to live there because I was accepted for whatever I was. In the hotel there is a fosterhood and a community feeling. It's a good thing.

cont. page 10

© Vanguard magazine

Transgender people faced serious housing and employment discrimination in the 1960s, forcing many to live in dangerous and impoverished neighborhoods. From Vanguard *magazine.*

never emerged as an effective organization and existed primarily on paper, regrouped as CATS (California Advancement for Transsexuals Society) under the leadership of Louise Ergestrasse. The divisions within COG may well have reflected the split between Kohler's more assimilationist, upwardly mobile mind-set and Ergestrasse's orientation toward transgender street subcultures. Far more successful than either was the National Transsexual Counseling Unit (NTCU), which, in 1968, brought together many of the players in San Francisco's mid-1960s transgender activist scene. The NTCU's success was due in large measure to the financial support provided to it by one of the most colorful figures in U.S. transgender history—wealthy female-to-male transsexual philanthropist Reed Erickson.

A Behind-the-Scenes Benefactor

Before Reed Erickson became an influential voice on transgender matters, most of the important figures in transgender political history were nontransgendered men and transgender women (though of course there were numerous transmen and masculine female-bodied people whose lives can be recovered from the historical record). A community of transmen would become increasingly organized, active, and visible by the 1970s; transgender men before Erickson, however, tended to disappear into the woodwork of mainstream society and tended not to participate in groups and organizations. One reason for this difference lay in the fact that it was often easier for a mature female to pass as a young man than it was for a mature male to pass as a woman (with or without the use of hormones and surgery). Because visually perceiving someone to be transgendered is one of the main triggers for antitransgender discrimination and violence, transgender women have been disproportionately affected by denials of employment and housing, and by violent crimes against them, and have had greater needs to take political and self-protective action. Transgender women who survive by participating in sexual street subcultures have long banded together for mutual support, whereas transgender men often lived without being part of a larger transgender community. As a result, the political history of transgender men and women, which has grown increasingly intertwined since the 1990s, sprang from very different sociological roots.

Reed Erickson, whose life has been extensively researched by Aaron Devor, was born female in El Paso, Texas in 1917 and grew up in Philadelphia, where his father owned a successful lead-smelting company. The family moved its business to Baton Rouge, Louisiana, in the late 1930s and became quite wealthy by selling lead to the state's petroleum industry for use as a fuel additive. Erickson was the first female graduate of Louisiana State University's Mechanical Engineering program and worked for several years during the mid-1940s as an engineer in Philadelphia, where he lived in an openly lesbian relationship and became active in left-wing political causes. As a consequence, Erickson came under FBI surveillance as a suspected communist and was reputedly blacklisted from several jobs. He returned to Baton Rouge in the early 1950s to work in family-owned businesses and start one of his own—a company that manufactured metal folding chairs and stadium bleacher seating. When his father died in 1962, Erickson inherited the family businesses and ran them successfully until selling them to Arrow Electronics in 1969 for roughly $5 million. Reed Erickson's personal fortune exceeded $40 million, which gave him the means to pursue many eccentric interests. In addition to being a successful businessman he was a nudist, New Age spiritualist, and recreational drug user. He flew his own planes, once sold his private yacht to Cuban revolutionary Fidel Castro, kept a pet leopard, believed in extrasensory perception and interspecies communication, and maintained a gated residential compound in Mazatlán, Mexico, that he named the Love Joy Palace. Erickson, who eventually became addicted to the powerful psychotropic drug ketamine and was under indictment in the United States on several drug-related charges, fled to the Love Joy Palace permanently in 1972; he died there in 1992 after many years of deteriorating physical and mental health.

Within a year of his father's death, Erickson had contacted Harry Benjamin and become his patient. He started masculinizing his body in 1963 and began to live socially as a man at that time. In 1964, he established the Erickson Educational Foundation (EEF) to support his many interests, as well as a separate foundation that specifically supported the work of Harry Benjamin, and a third entity, the Institute for the Study of Human Resources (ISHR), that quietly funded numerous other academic and medical research programs. The EEF developed a series of educational pamphlets that gave basic advice to transsexuals on such matters as how to legally change one's name or where to find a competent surgeon. It was Erickson's behind-the-scenes money that funded Benjamin to write *The Transsexual Phenomenon* and greased the wheels at prestigious educational institutions such as Johns Hopkins, Stanford, the University of Minnesota, UCLA, and the medical campus of the University of Texas on Galveston Island, all of which established major clinical research programs to study transgender and transsexual phenomena. Erickson was also a major benefactor of the ONE Institute, an educational organization that grew out of the homophile activist group in Los Angeles that published *ONE* magazine.

In funding the medical-legal-psychotherapeutic institutional framework within which transgender concerns have been addressed in the United States for more than forty years, Erickson pursued the same strategy pursued by the homophile organizations of the day—providing direct support to members of oppressed minority communities while marshaling the powers of social legitimation to speak about the issues in a new way. Although that model of activism (and the institutions it helped build) have come under criticism from later generations, Erickson seems to have accomplished what was possible for him to accomplish at the time. In spite of his wealth and great range of opportunity, he faced many of the same issues faced by other transgender people—such as being denied employment and having to educate his service providers about his own healthcare needs. The name Erickson chose for ISHR, his foundation

© Aaron Devor

Millionaire philanthropist Reed Erickson was a transman who funded the revolutions in transgender healthcare and social services that blossomed in the 1960s.

to promote the study of "human resources," was grounded in his own perception of having more potential for making a positive contribution to the world than circumstances would allow; he thought that transgender people such as himself represented a vastly underused resource of talent, creativity, energy, and determination. Although he was able to work on a scale that most people can only dream of, Erickson in fact did what most transgender people find themselves needing to do—working to create the conditions that allow them to get on with their lives.

Reed Erickson became aware of the unprecedented social and political developments in San Francisco through his close contact with Harry Benjamin, and after watching the situation there develop for a couple of years, he decided to fund the National Transsexual Counseling Unit. The EEF paid the rent and provided office furnishings for the NTCU, and it also paid the salaries of two full-time peer counselors, who did street outreach, provided walk-in counseling, and answered a steady stream of mail from gender-questioning people around the world. For the most part, the NTCU directed its clients to the Center for Special Problems for additional services. San Francisco police officer Elliott Blackstone, in an unusual administrative arrangement, managed the NTCU office as part of his responsibilities in the police community relations program but drew no salary from the EEF. Blackstone did, however, travel to police professional development meetings and criminal justice conferences in the United States and Europe at EEF's expense to promote his unusually critical views on police treatment of transgender people. At the NTCU office, he worked with individual transgender people to resolve conflicts they had with the law or with employers, and with social service agencies to encourage them to be more responsive to transgender needs. He also conducted sensitivity training on gay and transgender issues for every San Francisco Police Academy class. By the end of the 1960s, the combined efforts of politically mobilized transgender communities, sympathetic professionals, and public servants, and a generous infusion of private money made San Francisco the unquestioned hub of the transgender movement in the United States.

Stonewall

Meanwhile, across the continent, another important center of transgender activism was taking shape in New York City, where, not coincidentally, Harry Benjamin maintained his primary medical practice. In 1968, Mario Martino, a female-to-male transsexual, founded Labyrinth, the first organization in the United States devoted specifically to the needs of transgender men. Martino and his wife, who both worked in the healthcare field, helped other FTM transsexuals navigate their way through the often-confusing maze of transgender-oriented medical services just then beginning to emerge, which (despite being funded primarily by Reed Erickson) were geared more toward the needs of transgender women than transgender men. Labyrinth was not a political organization, but rather one that aimed to help individuals make the often-difficult transition from one social gender to another.

Far overshadowing the quiet work of Martino's Labyrinth Foundation, however, were the dramatic events of June 1969 at the Stonewall Inn, a gay bar in New York's Greenwich Village. The "Stonewall Riots" have been mythologized as the origin of the gay liberation movement, and there is a great deal of truth in that characterization, but as we have seen, gay, transgender, and gender-variant people had been engaging in violent protest and direct actions against social oppression for at least a decade by that time. Stonewall stands out as the biggest and most consequential example of a kind of event that was becoming increasingly common rather than as a unique occurrence. By 1969, as a result of many years of social upheaval and political agitation, large numbers of people who were socially marginalized because of their sexual orientation or gender identity, especially younger people who were part of the Baby Boom generation, were drawn to the idea of "gay revolution" and were primed for any event that would set such a movement off. The Stonewall Riots provided that very spark, and they inspired the formation of Gay Liberation Front cells in big cities, progressive towns, and college campuses all across the United States. Ever since the summer of 1969, various groups of people who identify with those who participated in the rioting have argued about what actually happened, what the riot's underlying causes were, who was most affected, and what the movements that point back to Stonewall as an important part of their own history have in common with one another.

Although Greenwich Village was not as economically down-and-out as San Francisco's Tenderloin, it was nevertheless a part of the city that appealed to the same sorts of people who resisted at Cooper's, Dewey's, and Compton's: drag queens, hustlers, gender nonconformists of many varieties, gay men, a smattering of lesbians, and countercultural types who simply "dug the scene." The Stonewall Inn was a small, shabby, Mafia-run bar (as were many of the gay-oriented bars in New York back in the days when homosexuality and cross-dressing were crimes). It drew a racially mixed crowd and was popular mainly for its location on Christopher Street near Sheridan Square, where many gay men "cruised" for casual sex, and because it featured go-go boys, cheap beer, a good jukebox, and a crowded dance floor. Police raids were relatively frequent (usually when the bar was slow to make its payoffs to corrupt cops) and relatively routine and uneventful. Once the bribes were sorted out, the bar would reopen, often on the same night. But in the muggy, early morning hours of Saturday, June 28, 1969, events departed from the familiar script when the squad cars pulled up outside the Stonewall Inn.

A large crowd of people gathered on the street as police began arresting workers and patrons and escorting them out of the bar and into the waiting paddy wagons. Some people started throwing coins at the police officers, taunting them for taking "payola." Eyewitness accounts of what happened next differ in their particulars, but some witnesses claim a butch lesbian resisted police attempts to put her in the paddy wagon, while others noted that African American and Puerto Rican members of the crowd—many of them queens, feminine gay men, or transgender women—grew increasingly angry as they watched their "sisters" being arrested and escalated the level of opposition to the police. Both stories might well be true. Sylvia Rivera, a transgender woman who came to play an important role in subsequent transgender

Radical Transsexual

Suzy Cooke was a young hippie from upstate New York who lived in a commune in Berkeley, California, when she started transitioning from male to female in 1969. She came out as a bisexual transsexual in the context of the radical counterculture.

I was facing being called back up for the draft. I had already been called up once and had just gone in and played crazy with them the year before. But that was just an excuse. I had also been doing a lot of acid and really working things out. And then December 31, 1968, I took something—I don't really know what it was—but everything just collapsed. I said, "This simply cannot go on." To the people that I lived with, I said, "I don't care if you hate me, but I'm just going to have to do something. I'm going to have to work it out over the next couple of months, and that it doesn't matter if you reject me, I just have to do it."

As it was, the people in my commune took it very well. I introduced the cross-dressing a few days later as a way of avoiding the draft. And they were just taken aback at how much just putting on the clothes made me into a girl. I mean, hardly any makeup. A little blush, a little shadow, some gloss, the right clothes, padding. I passed. I passed really easily in public. This is like a few months before Stonewall. And by this point I was dressing up often enough that people were used to seeing it.

I was wallowing in the happiness of having a lot of friends. Here I was being accepted, this kinda cool/sorta goofy hippie kid. I was being accepted by all these heavy radicals. I had been rejected by my parental family, and I had never found a family at college, and now here I was with this family of like eight people all surrounding me. And as it turned out, even some of the girls that I had slept with were thinking that this was really cool. All the girls would donate clothes to me. I really had not been expecting this. I had been expecting rejection, I really had been. And I was really very pleased and surprised. Because I thought that if I did this then I was going to have to go off and live with the queens. And I didn't.

political history, long maintained that she threw the beer bottle that tipped the crowd's mood from playful mockery to violent resistance, after she was jabbed by a police baton. In any case, the targeting of gender-variant people, people of color, and poor people during a police action would fit the usual patterns of police hostility in such situations.

Bottles, rocks, and other heavy objects were soon being hurled at the police, who began grabbing people in the crowd and beating them in retaliation. Weekend partiers and residents in the heavily gay neighborhood quickly swelled the ranks of the crowd to more than two thousand people, and the outnumbered police barricaded themselves inside the Stonewall Inn and called for reinforcements. Outside, rioters used an uprooted parking meter as a battering ram to try to break down the bar's door, while other members of the crowd attempted to throw a Molotov cocktail inside to drive the police back into the streets. Tactical Patrol Force officers arrived on the scene in an attempt to contain the growing disturbance, which nevertheless continued for hours until dissipating before dawn. The next night, thousands of people regrouped at the Stonewall Inn to protest; when the police arrived to break up the assembled crowd, street fighting even more violent than the night before ensued. One particularly memorable sight amid the melee was a line of drag queens, arms linked, dancing a can-can and singing campy, improvised songs that mocked the police and their inability to regain control of the situation. Minor skirmishes and protest rallies continued throughout the next few days before finally dying down. By that time, however, untold thousands of people had been galvanized into political action.

Stonewall's Transgender Legacy

Within a month of the Stonewall Riots, gay activists inspired by the events in Greenwich Village formed the Gay Liberation Front (GLF), which modeled itself on radical Third World liberation and anti-imperialist movements. The GLF spread quickly through activist networks in the student and antiwar movements, primarily among white young people of middle-class origin. Almost as quickly as it formed, however, divisions appeared within the GLF, primarily taking aim at the movement's domination by white men and its perceived marginalization of women, working-class people, people of color, and transgender people. A more conservative faction broke off and reorganized as the Gay Activists Alliance (GAA), which worked to reform laws rather than stir up revolution. Many lesbians redirected their energy toward radical feminism and the women's movement. And transgender people, after working to form the GLF (and being explicitly excluded from the GAA's agenda), quickly came to feel that they did not have a welcome place in the movement they had done much to inspire. As a consequence, they soon formed their own organizations.

In 1970, Sylvia Rivera and another veteran of the Stonewall Riots, Marsha P. Johnson, established STAR—Street Transvestite Action Revolutionaries. Their primary goal was to help kids on the street find food, clothing, and a place to live. They opened STAR House, an overtly politicized version of the "house" culture that already characterized black and Latino queer kinship networks, where dozens of transgender youth could count on a free and safe place to sleep. Rivera and Johnson, as "house mothers," would hustle to pay the rent, while their "children" would scrounge for food. Their goal was to educate and protect the younger people who were coming into the kind of life they themselves led—they even envisioned establishing a school for kids who'd never learned to read

© Amy Coleman

Marsha P. (for "Pay It No Mind") Johnson was a veteran of the 1969 Stonewall Riots in New York and cofounder, with Sylvia Rivera, of STAR—Street Transvestite Action Revolutionaries.

and write because their formal education was interrupted because of discrimination and bullying. Some STAR members, particularly Rivera, were also active in the Young Lords, a revolutionary Puerto Rican youth organization. One of the first times the STAR banner was flown in public was at a mass demonstration against police repression organized by the Young Lords in East Harlem in 1970, in which STAR participated as a group. STAR House lasted for two or three years and inspired a few short-lived imitators in other cities.

A few other transgender groups formed in New York in the early 1970s. A transsexual woman named Judy Bowen organized two extremely short-lived groups—Transvestites and Transsexuals (TAT) in 1970 and Transsexuals Anonymous in 1971—neither of which seems to have made any lasting impact. More significant was the Queens' Liberation Front (QLF), founded by drag queen Lee Brewster and heterosexual transvestite Bunny Eisenhower. The QLF formed in part to resist the erasure of drag and transgender visibility in the first Christopher Street Liberation Day march, which commemorated the Stonewall Riots and is now an annual event held in New York on the last Sunday in June. In many other cities, this weekend has become the traditional date to celebrate Gay Pride. The formation of the QLF demonstrates how quickly the gay liberation movement started to push aside some of the very people who had the greatest stake in militant resistance at Stonewall. QLF members participated in that first Christopher Street Liberation Day march and were involved in several other political campaigns through the next few years—including wearing drag while lobbying state legislators in Albany. QLF's most lasting contribution, however, was the publication of *Drag Queen* magazine (later simply *Drag*), which had the best coverage of transgender news and politics in the United States, and which offered fascinating glimpses of transgender life and activism outside the major cities. In New York, QLF founder Lee Brewster's private business, Lee's Mardi Gras Boutique, was a gathering place for the city's transgender community well into the 1990s.

Angela K. Douglas

One other burst of transgender activist energy during this period that deserves particular mention revolved around Angela K. Douglas. Douglas had been involved in the countercultural scene in Los Angeles in the mid-1960s, where she met many soon-to-be-famous filmmakers and rock musicians. She herself, before her transition in 1969, played in the obscure psychedelic rock band Euphoria. Douglas covered the birth of gay liberation politics for the Los Angeles underground press and joined GLF-LA, which she soon left because of the transphobia she perceived in that organization. (It should also be noted that Morris Kight, the principal architect of the gay liberation movement in Los Angeles, suspected Douglas to be an FBI informant.) She subsequently formed TAO (Transsexual Activist Organization) in 1970, which published the *Moonshadow* and *Mirage* newsletters—always interesting hodgepodges of eccentric political screeds, psychedelic art, photographs, activist news, and occult beliefs. TAO was the first truly international grassroots transgender community organization, with a worldwide mailing list and loosely affiliated chapters in various cities— including one in Birmingham, England, that shaped the sensibilities of FTM activist attorney Stephen Whittle, who would lead a successful campaign for transgender legal reform in the U.K. in the 1990s and establish himself as one of the leading international authorities on transgender legal and human rights issues.

Douglas, who suffered several psychotic breaks as a young adult, would spend most of her life living in poverty and ill health in rural Florida until her death in 2007. During this later period she wrote a poignant autobiography, *Triple Jeopardy* (self-published in 1982), penned a few songs, and churned out a prodigious amount of paranoid ravings directed at people she accused of "stealing her life." Throughout the 1970s, however, Douglas tirelessly crisscrossed the United States and wrote extensively for radical, countercultural, and transgender community publications. She was briefly involved in the New York radical sexuality scene, and her involvement there was mentioned in Donn Teal's as-it-happened history, *The Gay Militants*. Douglas moved her base of operations to Miami in 1972, where a significant part of TAO's membership was drawn from Cuban refugees and other Caribbean immigrants. She was always more of a gadfly and provocateur than a movement builder, and from her alternative perspective she ceaselessly criticized the doctors, lawyers, and psychiatrists associated with Harry Benjamin, the EEF, and the "police-run" NTCU in San Francisco. In spite of her growing psychiatric difficulties, Douglas's political writings offered important countercultural critiques of the emerging transgender establishment.

By the early 1970s transgender political activism had progressed in ways scarcely imaginable when the 1960s had begun. On one front, privileged white male transvestites were making community with one another in the nation's suburbs, while on another front, multiracial groups of militant cultural revolutionaries were claiming space for themselves in the streets of America's major cities. Transsexuals had taken the first crucial steps toward redefining the relationship between their needs and life goals and state-sanctioned medical care, social services, and legal accommodation of their identities. In spite of those remarkable accomplishments, however, the decade ahead would be one of the most difficult and frustrating periods of transgender history in the United States.

CHAPTER 4

THE DIFFICULT DECADES

By the early 1970s, American culture—especially popular culture—had undergone some startling transformations due to the upheavals of the 1960s. One of the most visible differences was a sudden proliferation of gender styles that broke free from the more rigid codes still in place in the early 1960s. In those earlier years, a woman wearing pants in public would still raise eyebrows, and a man with hair long enough to touch the collar of his shirt would be looked at with suspicion. After a decade of "sex, drugs, and rock and roll," more unisex fashions had become common, and there was a greater acceptance of traditionally masculine clothing on women. Men did not have the same license to embrace traditionally feminine clothing, but even so, society allowed them a greater range of expression in their appearance. On the cultural fringe, avant-garde transgender theatrical and musical acts such as the Cockettes and Sylvester (on the West Coast), and Wayne (later Jayne) County and the New York Dolls (on the East Coast), inspired the better-known gender-bending styles of glam rocker David Bowie and filmmaker John Waters's cult movie star Divine. High art and lowlife swirled around pop artist Andy Warhol's Factory, generating countercultural icons such as Lou Reed and the transgender Warhol superstars Candy Darling and Holly Woodlawn, infusing the glam, glitter, and early punk music scenes in venues such as Max's Kansas City and CBGB. For the first time in U.S. history, what could be described as a "transgender aesthetic," a new relationship between gendered appearance and biological sex, was becoming hip and cool for mass audiences. But these stylistic innovations did little to alter institutionalized forms of sexism and social oppression based on gender. Even as transgender styles began inching toward the cultural mainstream, people who lived transgender lives from day to day began to experience a profound backlash against the recent gains their community had made.

Backlash and Watershed

The transgender community was not alone in experiencing a political backlash. By the early 1970s, reactionary tactics by the government had violently shut down many countercultural tendencies that had emerged in the 1960s. The escalation of the war in Vietnam continued; antiwar activism and racial unrest roiled the streets of the nation from coast to coast, and the FBI's domestic surveillance program infiltrated many antiestablishment groups and movements. Members of the Black Panther Party were murdered by the police in Chicago, and antiwar student protesters were killed by National Guard troops at Kent State University in Ohio. In San Francisco during these years, a genital-mutilating serial killer began preying on transgender sex workers in the Tenderloin. Some transgender community members believed the killer or killers to be connected with the police vice squad, but these rumors were never substantiated, and no suspect was ever identified. Well documented, however, was the crippling of the National Transsexual Counseling Unit by reactionary members of the police department, who entrapped one of the peer counselors there in a drug bust. A police informant pretended to be sexually and romantically interested in the NTCU employee and then, after dating her for a few weeks, asked her to score cocaine for him and to bring it to work, where he would buy it from her. Once the drugs were on the premises, officers swooped in for the arrests. They also planted narcotics in Elliott Blackstone's desk, unsuccessfully attempting to frame him. The peer counselor was convicted on drug charges and spent two years in jail, and Blackstone, though he remained on the police force for a few more years until qualifying for his retirement pension, was reassigned to a new job in which he didn't interact with the city's transgender scene. The NTCU limped along for a while longer, but the agency (which renamed itself the Transexual Counseling Center, opting for the alternate spelling "transexual," using only one "s") closed in 1974, after losing its funding when the Erickson foundation wound down its operations.

The rise of university-based sex change programs during the late 1960s and early 1970s illustrates the complex cultural politics of transgender issues at this historical juncture. Some university-based research on transgender identification had been conducted at the University of California in the early 1950s, and the Gender Identity Research Clinic had been established on the UCLA campus in 1962. Within months of the publication of Harry Benjamin's *The Transsexual Phenomenon* in 1966, however, the Johns Hopkins University opened the first medical program in the United States to combine scientific research into the biology and psychology of gender with the expert evaluation of transgender individuals for hormone treatment and genital surgery. Similar programs quickly followed at the University of Minnesota, Stanford University, and the University of Texas's medical campus in Galveston, and still other programs developed at other universities and research hospitals in the years ahead. These years, between the mid-1960s and the late 1970s, represent what could be called the "Big Science" period of transgender history.

On the one hand, this heightened level of attention represented a welcome development for transgender citizens of the United States who wanted to physically change their sex. Before the development of these programs, U.S. trans people who sought surgery usually had to leave the country to find services overseas or in Latin America, and many simply could not afford to do so. These new programs, some of which were free of charge to qualified research participants, made "sex change" domestically available for the first time. On the other hand, as trans people seeking surgery and hormones quickly discovered, the new university-based scientific research programs were far more concerned with restabilizing the gender system, which seemed to be mutating all around them in bizarre and threatening directions, than

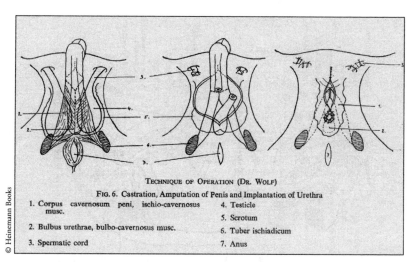

TECHNIQUE OF OPERATION (DR. WOLF)

FIG. 6. Castration, Amputation of Penis and Implantation of Urethra

1. Corpus cavernosum peni, ischio-cavernosus musc.

2. Bulbus urethrae, bulbo-cavernosus musc.

3. Spermatic cord

4. Testicle

5. Scrotum

6. Tuber ischiadicum

7. Anus

Medical drawing of a male-to-female genital conversion operation (1958), included in the text Homosexuality, Transvesticism, and Change of Sex, *by Eugene de Savitsch.*

they were in helping that cultural revolution along by further exploding mandatory relationships between sexed embodiment, psychological gender identity, and social gender role. Access to transsexual medical services thus became entangled with a socially conservative attempt to maintain traditional gender, in which changing sex was grudgingly permitted for the few of those seeking to do so, to the extent that the practice did not trouble the gender binary for the many.

The elaboration of an elite university-based medical research culture around "sex change" had significant consequences for transgender political activism. Transgenderism and homosexuality had been conceptually interrelated since the nineteenth century, and transgender politics, the homophile movement, and gay liberation had run alongside one another and sometimes intersected throughout the 1950s and '60s. The early 1970s, however, represented a watershed moment in this shared history when the transgender political movement lost its alliances with gay and feminist communities in ways that did not begin to be repaired until the early 1990s, and which, in many ways, have yet to be fully overcome. Although gay liberation and feminism are typically considered politically progressive developments, for transgender people they often constituted another part of the backlash, in large part because of the different relationships these movements and identities had to government policy and to institutionalized medical, scientific, and legal powers.

Consider, for example, how the course of the war in Vietnam affected gay male and transgender community dynamics. Direct U.S. involvement in Southeast Asian military conflicts began to escalate after the 1964 Gulf of Tonkin incident, in which communist North Vietnamese boats were accused of firing on the vessels of U.S. military advisers; major commitments of U.S. ground troops followed in 1965. The countercultural hippie style popular among both gays and straights—with its bright, flowing fabrics, long hair, and love beads—represented a deliberate reversal of the gender conventions of militaristic masculinity and signaled political opposition to the war. One popular sexual liberation slogan from the height of the antiwar movement was "Fuck, Don't Fight"; an unstated but equally apropos slogan for many draft-age men would have been "Genderfuck, Don't Fight." It should not be surprising that the period when male-to-female transgender people made their most significant political gains overlapped with a period in which public gender transgression by nontransgendered men had the broadest and deepest sense of political urgency. Significantly, however, when major U.S. involvement in Vietnam began to wind down, after the 1973 Paris Peace Accords, the gender coding of men's clothing styles simultaneously began to shift. In gay male culture, 1973 was the year that the masculine "clone look" of denim, plaid, and short haircuts replaced radical hippie/fairy chic, signaling the return of a more gender-normative expression of male homosexuality. At the cultural level, it is possible to trace the current "homonormativity" of mainstream gay culture (an emphasis on being "straight-looking and straight-acting"), as well as the perceived lack of meaningful connection to transgender communities among mainstream gays and lesbians, to the shifts of 1973.

Another marker of the growing divergence of transgender and

Trans Lib

In the early 1970s, trans people voiced their hopes for a liberation movement, using the same language and arguments that other liberation struggles drew from. Militant trans liberationists rejected the idea that they were simply enacting gender stereotypes and they resented the idea that they were expendable "shock troops" in feminist and gay liberation struggles. The following article, though it contains a few errors of historical fact, captures the spirit of early trans liberation sentiment; it documents both the nationwide scope of organizing and the perception among some trans people that their struggles were part of a larger movement for social change. The article originally appeared in 1971 in the *Trans Liberation Newsletter*.

Transvestite and Transsexual Liberation

The oppression against transvestites and transsexuals of either sex arises from sexist values and this oppression is manifested by homosexuals and heterosexuals alike in the form of exploitation, ridicule, harassment, beatings, rapes, murders and the use of us as shock troops and sacrificial victims.

We reject all labels of "stereotype," "sick," or "maladjusted" from non-transvestic and non-transsexual sources and defy any attempt to repress our manifestations as transvestites or transsexuals.

Trans Lib began in the summer of 1969 when Queens formed in New York and began militating for equal rights. In 1970 the Transvestite-Transsexual Action Organization (TACO) formed in Los Angeles, the Cockettes in San Francisco, Street Transvestite Action Revolutionaries (STAR) in New York, Fems Against Sexism and Transvestites and Transsexuals (TAT) also formed in New York. Radical Queens formed in Milwaukee—all in 1970. Queens became Queens Liberation Front.

Transvestism, transsexuality, and homosexuality are separate

homosexual communities can be seen in the campaign to depathologize homosexuality, which was considered a psychological illness in the United States until the early 1970s. Starting in the 1950s, homophile groups had worked with sympathetic straight or closeted members of the legal, medical, and psychiatric professions to delist it from the entities. Sexist values incorrectly classify any male who wears feminine attire as a homosexual, and to a lesser degree, any female who wears masculine attire is also classified as a homosexual.

We share in the oppression of Gay women. Trans Lib includes transvestites, transsexuals, and hermaphrodites of any sexual manifestation and of all sexes—heterosexuals, homosexual, bisexual, and asexual. It is becoming a separate movement as the great majority of transvestites are heterosexual, and many transsexuals (post-operative) are also heterosexual, and because the oppression directed toward us is due to our transvestism and transsexualism and for no other reason. We unite around our oppression, as all oppressed groups unite around their particular oppression. All power to Trans Liberation.

WE DEMAND
1. Abolition of all cross-dressing laws and restrictions of adornment.
2. An end to exploitation and discrimination within the gay world.
3. An end to exploitation practices of doctors and physicians in the fields of transvestism and transsexualism.
4. Free hormone treatment and surgery upon demand.
5. Transsexual assistance centers should be created in all cities with populations of one million inhabitants, under the direction of postoperative transsexuals.
6. Full rights on all levels of society and full voice in the struggles for liberation of all oppressed peoples.
7. Immediate release of all persons in mental hospitals or prison for transvestism or transsexualism.

Transvestites who exist as members of the opposite anatomical gender should be able to obtain full identification as members of the opposite gender. Transsexuals should be able to obtain such identification commensurate to their new gender with no difficulty, and not be required to carry special identification as transsexuals.

American Psychiatric Association's *Diagnostic and Statistical Manual of Mental Disorders (DSM)*. One of the first major accomplishments of the gay liberation movement that took shape in the wake of Stonewall was to achieve this long-term goal. Building on the foundation of homophile activism, gay psychologists who "came out" within their profession succeeded in having their peers remove homosexuality from the *DSM* in 1973. As a result, because gays were now "liberated" from the burden of psychopathology, homosexual and transgender communities no longer had a common interest in working to address how they were each treated by the mental health establishment. Gay liberationists who had little familiarity with transgender issues came to see transgender people as "not liberated" and lacking in political sophistication, as being still mired in an old-fashioned "preliberation" engagement with the establishment, as still trying to "fit in" with the system when what they should really be doing was freeing themselves from medical-psychiatric oppression.

In many respects, the transgender movement's politics toward the medical establishment were more like those of the reproductive freedom movement than those of the gay liberation movement. Transgender people, like people seeking abortions, wanted to secure access to competent, legal, respectfully provided medical services for a nonpathological need not shared equally by every member of society, a need whose revelation carried a high degree of stigma in some social contexts, and for which the decision to seek medical intervention in a deeply personal matter about how to live in one's own body was typically arrived at only after intense and often emotionally painful deliberation. The U.S. Supreme Court ruled on the landmark *Roe v. Wade* case in 1973, guaranteeing a woman's right to an abortion; transgender medical needs, however, were not viewed through the same set of rationales that won *Roe,* in large part because an emerging feminist position on transgender issues proved even more hostile to transgender interests than the gay liberation perspective.

The second wave of feminist activism in the United States is generally considered to have begun in the early 1960s, with the publication of Betty Friedan's *Feminine Mystique* in 1963 and the formation of the National Organization for Women (NOW) in 1966. Simone de Beauvoir's *Second Sex,* published in France in 1949, had prepared the ground by placing the question of feminism squarely at the forefront of post–World War II intellectual life. Early second wave feminism quickly came to be seen by those on the cultural and political left as white, middle class, heterosexual, and establishment oriented in its worldview, however, and more radical and countercultural versions of feminism critiqued the feminist mainstream almost from the beginning. New Yorker Robin Morgan played an important role in launching WITCH (Women's International Terrorist Conspiracy from Hell) in 1968, a loose network of socialist-feminist collectives, and her views would have a powerful influence on early radical feminist views of transgender issues. Also, shortly after the formation of the Gay Liberation Front in 1969, many lesbians associated with gay liberation began meeting in feminist consciousness-raising groups. One of these groups, the Radicalesbians, involving Rita Mae Brown, Karla Jay, and others, played a pivotal part in the political development of lesbian feminism through its influential pamphlet, "The Woman-Identified Woman."

At the second Conference to Unite Women, held in New York in 1970, the Radicalesbians and their paradigm-shifting pamphlet burst onto the scene in response to recent pejorative comments by Betty Friedan about the "lavender menace"—the question of lesbian participation in feminist politics. Friedan opposed associating lesbian concerns with feminism because she feared that society's homophobia would limit feminism's appeal and hamper its progress. The Radicalesbians staged what has come to be known as the "Lavender Zap" when, just as the conference was about to begin, they cut power to the microphones, killed the lights, and stormed the stage. When the lights came back up and the mics came back on a few moments later, Radicalesbian members wearing LAVENDER MENACE T-shirts had commandeered the attention of all present. They passed out copies of "The Woman-Identified Woman" and facilitated a discussion of feminism, homophobia, and lesbian baiting that changed the direction of feminist politics in the United States.

"The Woman-Identified Woman" famously begins with the statement, "A lesbian is the rage of all women condensed to the point of explosion." Its major conceptual accomplishment was to create linkages between straight and lesbian women through a shared understanding of gender oppression—for all feminist women, in other words, to be "woman-identified," to give strength to each other, rather than reflecting back to each other the "self-hate and the lack of real self" that were "rooted in our male-given identity" as patriarchally defined women. The idea of women's having their primary emotional ties to each other, regardless of their sexual orientation, rather than to men, was a major milestone in the historical development of feminist consciousness, as was the sense that gender roles were male defined and functioned strictly as a form of repression to keep women in a subordinate position relative to men.

As vital, however, as these moves were for nourishing an incipient feminist sense of pride and strength, and however much they cleared conceptual space for redefining and politicizing gender, they nevertheless also precipitated a significant recontextualization of some lesbian sexual subcultures, a development not necessarily beneficial for all concerned. The traditional organization of lesbian erotic life around "butch" and "femme" identities fell under suspicion as examples of "male identification" and "patriarchal gender" that pathetically imitated heterosexual male/female couplings, and that did not further the revolutionary goal of overthrowing gender itself. As a result, butches, who expressed an unwelcome masculinity, as well as femmes, who embraced a feminine gender presentation deemed politically reactionary, were marginalized within a lesbian feminist political community whose "androgynous" style was seen as gender neutral.

One consequence of this shift away from "roles" and toward androgyny in lesbian and feminist culture was the foreclosure of social space that tolerated female-bodied masculine-identified people (some of whom might now be characterized as transgender), along with the women who loved them, who had previously had a place in women's and lesbian communities. The erosion of that space directly influenced the formation of FTM (female-to-male) transgender communities by the middle years of the 1970s. Before pursuing that story, however, it seems important to document the emergence of new transphobic discourses based on gay liberation and lesbian feminist analyses of gender. Most of this discourse initially addressed male-to-female transsexuals who were involved in feminist communities, but, as the female-to-male community grew in the 1980s and '90s, older arguments were revised, expanded, and adapted to take greater account of female-bodied gender variance.

Feminist Transphobia

As the preceding paragraphs suggest, 1973 represented a low point in U.S. transgender political history. Trans people, when they transitioned from one gender to another, still routinely faced loss of family and friends, housing and employment discrimination, high levels of social stigma, and greater risks for experiencing violence. Long-standing antitransgender prejudices meshed with new levels of medical attention to make pathologization the readiest path to healthcare services and a better quality of life. Progressive political movements, rather than critiquing the medical system that told transgender people they were sick, instead insisted that transgender people were politically regressive dupes of the patriarchal gender system who, at best, deserved to have their consciousnesses raised. A "perfect storm" of hostility toward transgender issues was beginning to gather force.

Some transgender people of the post–World War II Baby Boom had been drawn to gay liberation, radical feminism, and New Left politics, just like many other members of their generation, but their welcome there tended to be short-lived. San Francisco's first Gay Pride parade in 1972 (which commemorated the Compton's Cafeteria riot along with Stonewall and welcomed drag participation) degenerated into fistfighting when the Reverend Raymond Broshears, one of the gay male organizers, punched members of a lesbian separatist contingent who insisted on carrying signs that said Off the Pricks! in violation of the parade's "no violence" policy. At the postparade rally, feminists and some of their gay male supporters denounced the fight as an example of stereotypical gender roles and patriarchal oppression of women, and they announced that they never again would participate in a gay pride event organized by Broshears, or in one that permitted drag queens to "mock" women. In 1973, two separate San Francisco Pride events were organized, one by Broshears, and the other by gays and lesbians who opposed drag and expressly forbid transgender people from participating. Broshears never subsequently organized another Gay Pride event, while the antidrag event became the forerunner of the current San Francisco LGBT Pride celebration. That same year, across the continent in New York, Stonewall veteran and STAR founder Sylvia Rivera was forcibly prevented from addressing the annual commemoration of Christopher Street Liberation Day. But perhaps the most consequential incident in the rising tide of hostility toward transgender people in the summer of 1973 was directed against transsexual lesbian singer Beth Elliott by Robin Morgan at the West Coast Lesbian Feminist Conference.

Beth Elliott discovered her feminism, lesbianism, and womanhood in the context of a college friendship in the late 1960s with a young woman who was also in the process of coming out. After transitioning from male to female in her late teens, Elliott subsequently threw herself into community activism by participating in the hippie folk music scene, becoming an antiwar activist, and serving as vice president of the San Francisco chapter of the pioneering lesbian organization the Daughters of Bilitis. Her formative teenage relationship came back to haunt her in the early 1970s, however, when her former college friend, by now a member of the lesbian separatist Gutter Dykes Collective, publicly accused Elliott of having sexually harassed her years earlier—a charge Elliott vigorously and vehemently denied, but which, by the very nature of things, could never be extricated from the circular round of "she said/she said" accusations, denials, and counteraccusations. In retrospect, these accusations of harassment appear to be an early instance—perhaps the first—of an emerging discourse in feminism that held all male-to-female transsexuals to be, by definition, violators of women, since they represented an "unwanted penetration" into women's space. Elliott, for her part, claims her former friend made false accusations to save face within her separatist clique once her adolescent friendship with Elliott became known, but whatever the circumstances might have been, the public accusation of sexual misconduct served as a lightning rod for discharging years of gathering unease about the participation of transgender women in lesbian space. It devastated Elliott, derailed her career in the early women's movement and music scene, and became the basis for one of the most pernicious and persistent characterizations of transgender people to be found in all of feminism.

The fallout began in December 1972 when Elliott was ousted from the Daughters of Bilitis, not because of any accusations against her but on the grounds that she wasn't "really" a woman; several other members resigned in protest over that decision. Meanwhile, Elliott also served on the organizing committee of the West Coast Lesbian Feminist Conference, planned for April of 1973 in Los Angeles, and she had been asked to perform as a singer in the conference's entertainment program. The Gutter Dykes leafleted the conference to protest the presence there of a "man" (Elliott), and keynote speaker Robin Morgan, recently arrived from the East Coast, hastily expanded her address to incorporate elements

Transsexual lesbian singer and activist Beth Elliott in the 1970s.

of the brewing controversy. All of her incorporations seem to have come from separatist material, and none from Elliott and her supporters. Morgan's speech, titled "Lesbianism and Feminism: Synonyms or Contradictions?" was subsequently published in her memoir *Going Too Far: The Personal Chronicle of a Feminist*, and it was also widely anthologized. More than twelve hundred women at the conference—which turned out to be the largest lesbian gathering to date—listened to the speech firsthand. For many attendees, the controversy over Beth Elliott's participation in the West Coast Lesbian Feminist Conference was their first encounter with the "transgender question," and what transpired there would inform opinions nationwide.

"All hell broke loose that very first night, caused by the gate-crashing presence of a male transvestite who insisted that he was 1) an invited participant, 2) really a woman, and 3) at heart a lesbian," Morgan wrote in the introductory notes to *Going Too Far*. "It was incredible that so many strong angry women should be divided by one smug male in granny glasses and an earth-mother gown." In the 1973 speech itself, Morgan asked her audience why some of them felt compelled to defend the "obscenity of male transvestism" and to "permit into our organizations . . . men who deliberately *re*emphasize gender roles, and who parody female oppression and suffering." "No," she continued, displaying her inability to distinguish between male-to-female transsexual life contexts and episodic gay drag or heterosexual cross-dressing: "I will not call a male 'she'; thirty-two years of suffering in this androcentric society and of surviving, have earned me the title 'woman'; one walk down the street by a male transvestite, five minutes of his being hassled (which he may enjoy), and then he dares, he dares to think he understands our pain? No, in our mothers' names and in our own, we must not call him sister."

Morgan then went on to identify Elliott as "the same man who four years ago tried to pressure a San Francisco lesbian into letting him rape her; the same man who single-handedly divided and almost destroyed the San Francisco Daughters of Bilitis Chapter." She accused Elliott of "leeching off women who have spent entire lives *as women* in women's bodies" and ended her personal attack by declaiming: "I charge him as an opportunist, an infiltrator, and a destroyer—with the mentality of a rapist." Morgan then called upon the conference attendees to vote on ejecting Elliott, saying, "You can let him into your workshops—or you can *deal* with him." According to writers for the *Lesbian Tide,* more than two-thirds of those present voted to allow Elliott to remain, but the antitranssexual faction refused to accept the popular results and promised to disrupt the conference if their demands were not met. Eventually, after much rancorous debate, Beth Elliott went on to perform but thereafter left the remainder of the conference.

Conference attendees brought news of the Elliott controversy (and of course much else) back to women's communities across the country, and, throughout the middle years of the 1970s, the "transsexual rapist" trope began to circulate in grassroots lesbian networks as the most extreme version of an antipathy toward transgender people rooted in the concepts of "woman identification" and "women-only space." In 1977, for example, Sandy Stone, a male-to-female transsexual recording engineer who had worked with Jimi Hendrix and other rock luminaries before joining the Olivia Records collective to help launch the women's music industry, became the target of an antitranssexual campaign among some women who threatened to boycott Olivia if Stone did not resign, arguing that consumers were being deceived in the claim that Olivia was "women-only." Although the collective was willing to stick by Stone on principle, she voluntarily left to pursue other opportunities in order not to damage Olivia's business. By 1978, Boston University feminist theologian Mary Daly had elevated transphobia to a metaphysical precept by labeling transsexuality a "necrophilic invasion" of vital women's space in the section of her book, *Gyn/Ecology,* called "Boundary Violation and the Frankenstein Phenomenon." But it was Daly's doctoral student, Janice G. Raymond, who, in 1979, consolidated the many strands of antitransgender discourse circulating within the feminist community into one grand narrative, published as *The Transsexual Empire: The Making of the She-Male.*

Because Raymond's book has played such an important role in transgender political history—serving both as a sourcebook for antitransgender opinion and a goad for transgender theorizing—it merits discussion here at some length. As the debates about transgender issues have shifted during the 1990s and the 2000s, Raymond's attitudes—never representative of all feminist opinion—have been caricatured and derided by people friendly to transgender concerns, while those hostile to transgender interests hold her work up as a sound argument in their favor, sometimes without having actually read her book. Because what she actually wrote has been obscured by the heated arguments of others, and because her own arguments continue to be referenced in contemporary community debates, it seems useful to quote Raymond extensively.

First, Raymond explicitly identifies the practice of transsexuality with rape, unequivocally stating: "All transsexuals rape women's bodies by reducing the real female form to an artifact, appropriating this body for themselves"; she asserts that the mere presence of male-to-female transsexuals in women's space "violates women's sexuality and spirit." Rape, she claims, is usually accomplished by force, but it can also be accomplished by deception; male-to-female transsexuals who seek to be involved in women's and feminist communities "merely cut off the most obvious means of invading women," but they continue to rape women, as she claims Sandy Stone did via her work at Olivia, whenever they do not declare themselves to be transsexuals.

Furthermore, Raymond claims that male-to-female transsexuals are agents of the patriarchal oppression of women, comparing them to the eunuchs (castrated males) who once guarded the harem tents for Eastern potentates. "Will the acceptance of transsexually constructed lesbian-feminists who have lost only the outward appendages of their physical masculinity lead to the containment and control of lesbian-feminists?" Raymond asks. "Will every lesbian-feminist space become a harem?" Just because some "men" are castrated doesn't make them "un-men," she continues; it just means they can be used as "'keepers' of woman-identified women when the 'real men,' the 'rulers of patriarchy,' decide that the women's movement . . . should be controlled and contained." In this way, she claims, eunuchs, too, "can rise in the Kingdoms of the Fathers." Combining Orientalist stereotypes with a thinly veiled Islamophobia, Raymond thus constructs the transsexual as a tool of alien powers bent on the subjugation of progressive Western feminism.

One of the more lurid yet logically incoherent sections of *The Transsexual Empire* is called "Learning from the Nazi Experience." "In mentioning the Nazi experiments," Raymond writes, "it is not my purpose to directly compare transsexual surgery to what went on in the camps but rather to demonstrate that much of what went on there can be of value in surveying the ethics of transsexualism." She then constructs a string of false syllogisms, inferences, and analogies that work to associate transsexuality with Nazism without actually asserting that transsexuals are Nazis or Nazi collaborators. Raymond quotes countercultural antipsychiatry guru Thomas Szasz to the effect that sometimes profit-hungry doctors have collaborated with governments and corporations in ways that seem to violate their professional ethics to "first do no harm," and then she notes that Nazi science was government funded. "Not so incidentally," she points out, "some transsexual research has been funded by government grants." Nazi doctors conducted experiments such as comparing the skulls of Aryans and non-Aryans to gain racial knowledge, whereas doctors in the 1970s experimented on transsexual bodies to learn whether it was "possible to construct a functional vagina in a male body" to gain sexual knowledge; therefore, Raymond claims, "What we are witnessing in the transsexual context is a science at the service of patriarchal ideology of sex-role conformity in the same way that breeding for blond hair and blue eyes became a so-called science at the service of Nordic racial conformity." The section ends with a series of statements and inferences bearing no logical relationship to one another: The Nazis were Germans; the first physician on record to perform a sex conversion surgery was a German who worked at Hirschfeld's institute in Germany; Harry Benjamin, a German, visited the Hirschfeld institute many times in the

Trans-Positive Second Wave Feminism

Second wave feminism was not uniformly hostile to transgender and transsexual people. Shulamith Firestone, a socialist feminist, was involved in some of the same radical feminist groups as Robin Morgan but broke with her over a number of political differences. Firestone took a different stance on the relationship between feminism and biomedical science from the views presented by Janice Raymond in *The Transsexual Empire*. In her book, *The Dialectic of Sex: A Case for Feminist Revolution*, Firestone wrote:

> *Just as to assure elimination of economic classes requires the revolt of the underclass (the proletariat) and . . . their seizure of the means of production, so to assure the elimination of sexual classes requires the revolt of the underclass (women) and the seizure of control of reproduction. . . . And just as the end goal of socialist revolution was not only the elimination of the economic class privilege but of the economic class distinction itself, so the end goal of feminist revolution must be, unlike that of the first feminist movement, not just the elimination of male privilege but of the sex distinction itself. . . . The reproduction of the species by one sex for the benefit of both would be replaced by (at least the option of) artificial reproduction: children would be born to both sexes equally, or independently of either.*

In the controversy about Beth Elliott's participation at the West Coast Lesbian Feminist Conference, *Lesbian Tide* publisher Jeanne Cordova drew parallels between antitransgender prejudice and other forms of

1920s; the institute's confidential files reputedly held compromising information on prominent homosexual or cross-dressing Nazis; and Nazis conducted medical experiments in the concentration camps that sometimes involved castration and hormone treatments aimed at "curing" homosexuality. Therefore? Transsexuality has something to do with Nazism.

Raymond, who has just spent so many words condemning eugenic arguments, begins the "Suggestions for Change" appended to her book discrimination such as sexism, homophobia, and racism. She and lesbian activist the Reverend Freda Smith of Sacramento "stepped up," in the words of Candy Coleman, to speak "loud and strong in defense of Beth Elliott"; Coleman, who identified herself as a "Gaysister," deplored the attacks on Elliott, whom she considered "right-on" and of whom she said, "I, like so many other women and Gaysisters, are proud to call her sister."

Deborah Feinbloom and her colleagues wrote an article for the *Journal of Homosexuality*, "Lesbian/Feminist Orientation Among Male-to-Female Transsexuals," in which they interviewed transgender women involved in lesbian feminism and found them to be not significantly different from nontranswomen in their political beliefs, activist philosophies, and gender ideology.

In the controversy about Sandy Stone's involvement with the all-women Olivia Records collective, C. Tami Weyant wrote to the feminist publication *Sister* and asserted that asking both MTF and FTM transsexuals to struggle against male privilege "as part of their feminist consciousness" was "fair," but that "rejecting them as transsexuals, period, will make us part of the oppression. . . . I strongly believe," she noted, "that only feminism can offer them safe harbor from that oppression, and that the shared issues they have struggled with demand that we struggle to accept all transsexuals who desire to be feminist."

As the foregoing statements suggest, there was nothing monolithic about second wave feminist attitudes toward trans issues. The feminist second wave simultaneously espoused some of the most reactionary attitudes toward trans people to be found anywhere while also offering a vision of transgender inclusion in progressive feminist movements for social change.

with the statement: "I contend that the problem of transsexualism would best be served by morally mandating it out of existence." She does not want to actually outlaw transsexual surgeries but rather to control and limit access to them (the way one would regulate methadone access to heroin addicts) and to promote legislation against sex-role stereotyping, "where it would be possible for the law to step in at the beginning of a destructive sexist process that leads ultimately to consequences such as transsexualism." In *The Transsexual Empire* and related presentations shortly after its publication, Raymond further recommended gender reorientation for transsexuals by means of feminist consciousness-raising therapy, which would explore "the social origins of the transsexual problem and the consequences of the medical-technical solution," and public education campaigns in which ex-transsexuals would speak of their dissatisfactions with changing sex, and in which former providers of medical services to transsexuals would discuss why they decided to stop providing services.

Transgender community members have asked since the 1970s how anyone could fail to see that Raymond's rhetoric and policy recommendations replicate arguments made by ex-gay ministries, antiabortion activists, bigots, and fearmongers of many stripes. In spite of these protestations, antitransgender discourses continued to proliferate in the 1980s, when it became common to denounce transsexuality as a "mutilating" practice and, if anything, the level of vitriol directed against transgender people actually increased. A 1986 letter to the editor published in the San Francisco lesbian newspaper *Coming Up* captures the vehemence with which transsexuals could be publicly vilified:

> One cannot change one's gender. What occurs is a cleverly manipulated exterior: what has been done is mutation. What exists beneath the deformed surface is the same person who was there prior to the deformity. People who break or deform their bodies [act] out the sick farce of a deluded, patriarchal approach to nature, alienated from true being. . . . When an estrogenated man with breasts loves women, that is not lesbianism, that is mutilated perversion. [Such an individual] is not a threat to the lesbian community, he is an outrage to us. He is not a lesbian, he is a mutant man, a self-made freak, a deformity, an insult. He deserves a slap in the face. After that, he deserves to have his body and his mind made well again.

Raymond herself has remained completely convinced of the correctness of her position. When *The Transsexual Empire* was reissued in 1994, with a "New Introduction on Transgender," Raymond reasserted her key points that "transsexualism constitutes a sociopolitical program that is undercutting the movement to eradicate sex-role stereotyping and oppression," that transsexuals are "so alienated from their bodies that they think little of mutilating them," and that accepting transsexual people as members of the social genders they live in and are perceived to be by others amounts to collusion with a "falsification of reality." When transgender people accuse some feminists of transphobia, it is to attitudes and statements such as these that they refer.

GID and HIV

Medical attention to transgender issues culminated in the creation of a new category of psychopathology, Gender Identity Disorder (GID), which was first listed in the fourth revised edition of the American Psychiatric Association's *Diagnostic and Statistical Manual of Mental Disorders* in 1980—the first edition published after the 1973 version that had removed homosexuality. The move toward creating this new category had begun many years earlier with the work of Harry Benjamin. In 1966, after the publication of *The Transsexual Phenomenon,* Benjamin's friends and colleagues had organized HBIGDA—the Harry Benjamin International Gender Dysphoria Association ("dysphoria," the opposite of "euphoria," being a term that meant "unhappiness"). HBIGDA became the main organization for medical, legal, and psychotherapeutic professionals who worked with transgender populations, and its membership consisted primarily of the surgeons, endocrinologists, psychiatrists, and lawyers affiliated with the big university-based programs that provided transgender healthcare and conducted research into gender identity formation. By the later 1970s, a decade of research had produced a set of treatment protocols for transgender patients, called the "Standards of Care," as well as a set of diagnostic criteria, which became formalized as GID.

With the "problem" of transsexuality now seemingly solved and contained, several of the university-based programs—notably the one at Johns Hopkins—closed down, and those at several other universities—such as Stanford—spun off into privately run clinics operated by doctors affiliated with the universities' medical schools. Responsibility for ensuring that professional standards of care were being met devolved onto a second tier of psychotherapists in private practice who were members of HBIGDA. Thus, by 1980, a routine set of procedures and protocols for medically managing transgender populations had fallen into place. A person seeking to change genders would need several months of psychotherapy for a diagnosis of GID before being referred to an endocrinologist for hormone therapy, followed by at least a year of living socially as a member of the desired gender. At that point, a psychiatrist would evaluate the suitability of the person seeking to change gender for surgery, after which legal changes in gender identity could be pursued.

As mentioned earlier, the construction of transgender identity as an official psychopathology recognized by accredited expert medical opinion would presumably mean that medical treatment of transsexuality would be considered a fully legitimate healthcare need. This proved, however, not to be the case. Insurance companies continued to consider transsexual healthcare treatments to be "experimental," "cosmetic," or "elective" and therefore ineligible for insurance coverage or reimbursement. Transgender access to government-funded social services, which had been more readily available during the Democratic administrations of Johnson and Carter, was drastically curtailed under Reagan—in part, it seems, in response to antitransgender feminist arguments that dovetailed with conservative politics. When antipornography feminists in this period, such as Catharine MacKinnon and Andrea Dworkin, allied themselves with conservative government policies in order to criminalize pornography (which they considered, often with some justification, to constitute violence against women), Janice Raymond hammered home the connections with transgender issues by suggesting that the "same socialization that enables men to objectify women in rape, pornography, and 'drag' enables them to objectify their own bodies," treating a penis a thing to "get rid of" and a vagina as something to acquire.

In briefly tracing the history of the emergence of GID, it is possible to see how the social power of science shifted, during the course of a few years in the 1970s, from a concern with sexual orientation to a preoccupation with gender identity. To a certain degree, the effectiveness of gay liberation and the successes of lesbian and gay civil rights activism had made it politically impossible for responsible medical professionals to continue treating homosexuality as a mental illness. At the same time, the success of feminism in destabilizing conventional means of social control over women's bodies made gender—rather than sexuality—into an even more important social battleground. The intensified interest of medical science in trying to understand, engineer, and "fix" gender in these years needs to be seen, in part, as an attempt to stuff the feminist genie back into its bottle. The result, for transgender people, was a lose-lose situation. All across the political spectrum, from reactionary to progressive and all points in between, the only options presented to them were to be considered bad, sick, or wrong. Consequently, transgender communities became very inwardly focused by the 1980s. They tended to concentrate more on providing mutual aid and support to their members than on broader social activism.

On top of this dismal situation, a devastating new threat to transgender communities appeared in 1981—the first visible manifestation of the AIDS pandemic. Transgender populations that relied on sex work for survival, that shared needles for injecting hormones, or that participated in the gay male sexual subcultures where the epidemic first gained widespread attention in the United States were especially hard-hit. Poor access to healthcare services due to poverty, stigma, and social isolation, as well as additional barriers to access created by the fear many transgender people have of disclosing their transgender status to healthcare providers (which could potentially reexpose them to social vulnerabilities they had worked hard to overcome), only served to compound the problem. As a result, the transgender community—especially poor, transgender women of color—now suffers one of the highest HIV infection rates in the world.

FTM Communities

F→M

The shifts in lesbian and feminist gender ideology that focused on "woman identification" and provided the conceptual underpinnings for some women to engage in transphobic attacks also encouraged some former butches and femmes to maintain the erotic dynamics of their relationships by leaving the homosexual subcultures they had once considered home and to blend into the dominant heteronormative population once the former butch had transitioned to life as a man. This is not to suggest that transmen would be lesbians given the opportunity but rather to point out that as one possible way of life for masculine-identified female-bodied people was becoming less available, other possibilities were expanding. These changes in the cultural landscape unavoidably affected the life paths many gender-questioning people followed. It's also important to note that not all FTMs have a lesbian history, and that many female-bodied people who were oriented toward men also found their way into female-to-male communities in increasing numbers by the mid-1970s and sometimes embraced gay male identities as they continued to be involved with men after transitioning. Jude Patton, with the Renaissance group in Los Angeles, and Rupert Raj of Toronto, with his *Metamorphosis* magazine, provided support for hundreds of transmen in the 1970s and '80s. In 1977, their fellow trans activist Mario Martino's memoir, *Emergence,* became the first full-length autobiography of an FTM man to be published in the United States, and it helped create even more visibility for transgender men.

One of the first pieces of media attention to draw attention to civil injustices encountered by transmen—and thus a key moment in the politicization of the FTM community—involved Steve Dain, an award-winning former high school physical education teacher in Emeryville,

California. In 1976, Dain had informed his principal that he would be transitioning genders during the school's summer vacation, and he asked to be reassigned to teach science rather than girls' gym. The request was granted, but because of a change in the school's administration, a new vice principal was unaware of Dain's plan. During the first day of classes, the administrator panicked when he learned that the new science teacher was none other than the old PE teacher, and he had Dain arrested in his classroom for "disturbing the peace." Dain successfully sued the Emeryville school district for a large but undisclosed sum and subsequently left teaching to pursue a career as a chiropractor. He became a highly visible spokesperson for FTM issues, appearing in the 1985 HBO documentary *What Sex Am I?* and serving as a lay counselor for many gender-questioning female-bodied people.

One of Dain's most significant protégés was Lou Sullivan, who became the hub of the organized FTM community in the United States in the 1980s. Born in 1951, Sullivan started keeping a journal as a ten-year-old girl growing up in the Milwaukee suburbs and continued journaling regularly until a few days before his untimely death at age thirty-nine, in 1991. In his journal Sullivan described his early childhood thoughts of being a boy, his confusing adolescent sexual fantasies of being a gay man, and his teenage participation in Milwaukee's countercultural music scene. He read John Rechy's novels and dreamed of running away to live with the drag queens of Los Angeles. By the time he graduated high school, he was dressing in men's clothes and was active in the Gay People's Union (GPU) at the University of Wisconsin—Milwaukee, where he found a job as a secretary in the Slavic Languages department.

By 1973, Sullivan self-identified as a "female transvestite" who was sexually attracted to gay and bisexual men. That same year, he launched a career of transgender community activism with the publication of "A Transvestite Answers a Feminist," an article that appeared in the *GPU News,* in which he recounted his conversations with a coworker who was critical of his cross-dressing. The argument Sullivan laid out— that all people represent their sense of themselves to others by means

Lou Sullivan: Recording a Life

Lou Sullivan's journals constitute one of the most complete, and one of the most compelling, accounts of a transgender life ever set to page. These excerpts, from ages eleven to twenty-two, chart the trajectory of his emerging gay male identity.

When we got home, we played boys.

—January 6, 1963, age eleven

My problem is that I can't accept life for what it is, like it's presented to me. I feel that there is something deep and wonderful underneath it that no one has found.

—December 12, 1965, age fourteen

No one looks deeper than the flesh.

—February 22, 1966, age fourteen

I want to look like what I am but don't know what someone like me looks like. I mean, when people look at me I want them to think, there's one of those people . . . that has their own interpretation of happiness. That's what I am.

—June 6, 1966, age fifteen

My heart and soul is with the drag queens. This last week or so I've wanted to go and leave everything and join that world. But where do I fit in? I feel so deprived and sad and lost. What can become of a girl whose real desire and passion is with male homosexuals? That I want to be one? I still yearn for that world, that world I know nothing about, a serious, threatening, sad, ferocious stormy, lost world.

—November 22, 1970, age nineteen

I know now that I can get exactly what I want—to fantasize is no longer enough. Before it was beyond my dreams. It was the worst perversion that I wished I had a penis, to fuck a boy, to be on top and inside! But now it's only a matter of time.

—December 11, 1973, age twenty-two

of certain recognizable gender conventions, and that transgender representations of masculine or feminine identities are no more nor no less "stereotypical" than those of anyone else—anticipated a line of thinking that became well established in transgender community discourses in the decades ahead. Another article, "Looking Towards Transvestite Liberation," published in the *GPU News* in 1974, was widely reprinted in the gay and lesbian press and remains a landmark article on the topic. Sullivan continued to contribute reviews and articles to the *GPU News* through 1980, many of them historical vignettes of female-bodied people who lived their lives as men. In doing so, he became an important community-based historian of FTM experience.

Sullivan had come to self-identify as a female-to-male transsexual by 1975, and he moved to San Francisco to seek sex reassignment at the Stanford University gender dysphoria program. He found work, as a female, as a secretary for the Wilson Sporting Goods Company,

Lou Sullivan, the leading organizer of the female-to-male (FTM) community in the 1980s.

but he spent most of his time cross-dressed as a young man, cruising the Castro neighborhood's gay enclave for anonymous sex. In 1976, Sullivan was rejected by the Stanford program on the basis of his openly declared gay male identity and spent the next four years continuing to live as a woman. During these years, in which he tried to make peace with his female embodiment, he participated in feminist consciousness-raising sessions (where he admits he worked through some internalized misogyny but never wavered in his gay male identity), learned to repair cars in an effort to combat limiting female stereotypes, and became active in San Francisco Bay Area MTF cross-dresser groups, where he worked to develop peer support for female-to-male individuals. Sullivan had read and been inspired by the 1976 newspaper coverage of Steve Dain's tribulations, but he first had a chance to meet his hero in 1979, after meeting a psychotherapist who happened to know Dain at a cross-dresser support organization.

Steve Dain offered Sullivan important validation and encouraged him to pursue transitioning if it was what he really wanted to do. By 1979, as noted earlier, the framework for transgender medical services was shifting away from university-based research programs and becoming considerably more decentralized. As a result, Sullivan was able to find psychotherapists, endocrinologists, and surgeons in private practice who were not concerned with his identification as a gay man and who were willing to help him transition. Sullivan started hormones in 1979, had chest surgery in 1980, and thereafter starting living full-time as a man. At this point, he threw himself even more fully into transgender community activism. He volunteered as the first FTM peer counselor at the Janus Information Facility, a private organization that took over the Erickson Educational Foundation's transgender information and referral activities after the Transexual Counseling Service folded. As a result, he found himself in contact with a multitude of gender-questioning female-bodied people from around the English-speaking world.

Sullivan simultaneously redoubled his efforts as a community-based historian. He gathered the vignettes he had published through the years in the *GPU News* and incorporated them into the guidebook he developed based on his work at Janus, *Information for the Female-to-Male Cross-Dresser and Transsexual*, which remained an essential guide for the FTM community well into the 1990s. In 1986, Sullivan became a founding member (and newsletter editor) of the Gay and Lesbian Historical Society (now the GLBT Historical Society), whose archives now comprise one of the best collections of material on gay, lesbian, bisexual, and transgender history anywhere in the world. As a result of Sullivan's early involvement, the organization's transgender holdings are particularly rich. Sullivan also started work on a book-length biography of Jack B. Garland, a nineteenth-century San Franciscan who had been born female but lived as a man in the Tenderloin, and who eroticized his relationships with the young men he met there and whom he helped out by offering food, shelter, and gifts of money. Eventually published in 1990, Sullivan's book argued that, contrary to the then-prevailing wisdom in gay and feminist scholarship, Garland did not live as a man to escape the conventional limitations of womanhood but because of his identification as a man and his homoerotic attraction to other men.

In 1986, while Sullivan was working to establish the GLBT archives in San Francisco, he also organized the first FTM-only support and education organization in the United States. Called simply "FTM," the organization held monthly "FTM Gatherings," featuring educational programs and opportunities to socialize, and also published the *FTM Newsletter*, which quickly became the leading source of information in the nation for female-to-male issues. Because of Sullivan's leadership role and his own gay identity, the San Francisco FTM group has always attracted a sexually diverse core membership and has avoided many of the divisions that had plagued similar MTF organizations since the 1960s. This openness was reflected in the newsletter's editorial slant and helped shape group sensibilities in the community of transmen that started blossoming in the 1980s under Sullivan's guidance. That organization became FTM International, the largest FTM group in the world; its San Francisco chapter is now called the Lou Sullivan Society.

Lou Sullivan's life tragically was cut short by an opportunistic illness contracted as a result of AIDS. It's likely that Sullivan became HIV-infected in 1980, just after his chest surgery, when he first felt comfortable visiting gay sex clubs; his diaries that summer record what he thought was a bad case of the flu, but which in retrospect was probably the moment when his body first started trying to fight off the HIV infection. He apparently remained asymptomatic for several years, until 1986, when complications from his genital surgery severely stressed his immune system. In the course of his long postsurgical recovery, Sullivan suddenly developed Pneumocystis carinii pneumonia, an especially virulent form of pneumonia closely associated with AIDS. At the time that his diagnosis was confirmed, survival rates for people with AIDS averaged somewhere in the vicinity of three years. Sullivan survived for five, in reasonably good health until the very end. In his final years he participated in AIDS drug trials, finished his book on Jack Garland, and continued to nurture the FTM group and the Historical Society. Sullivan's final campaign, however, was to persuade HBIGDA members and the committee revising the definition of GID for the next edition of the *Diagnostic and Statistical Manual* to drop "homosexual orientation" as a contraindication in the diagnostic criteria, which held that homosexual transgender people did not exist. Sullivan did not live to see that change take place in 1994, but he took comfort in knowing that his efforts were contributing to a revision of the sexological literature.

In one of his journal entries after his AIDS diagnosis, Lou mused about writing to the staff of the Stanford gender dysphoria program to say, "You told me I couldn't live as a gay man, but now I am going to die like one." He died in the company of friends and family on March 6, 1991, just as a new phase of transgender history was beginning to erupt.

CHAPTER 5

THE CURRENT WAVE

THE TREMENDOUS BURST OF NEW TRANSGENDER activism that began around 1990 came on the heels of a generally dispiriting decade or two, in which the transgender community made only small, erratic strides toward a better collective existence. A number of states, for example, eventually came to recognize legal change of sex on birth certificates, change of name and gender on driver's licenses, and the rights of postoperative transsexuals to marry in their preferred gender. A few (Illinois, Arizona, and Louisiana) had done so as early as the 1960s; several others (Hawaii, California, Connecticut, Massachusetts, Michigan, New Jersey, Virginia, North Carolina, and Iowa) had followed suit in the 1970s; and several more (Colorado, Arkansas, Georgia, Missouri, New Mexico, Oregon, Utah, Wisconsin, and the District of Columbia) had done so by the 1980s. In addition, three municipalities—Minneapolis, Minnesota; Harrisburg, Pennsylvania; and Seattle, Washington—had enacted human and civil rights protections for transgender people before the end of the 1980s. The Transsexual Rights Committee had formed in 1980 within the Southern California chapter of the American Civil Liberties Union (ACLU), and it had won a few modest victories pertaining to the treatment of trans people by the Veterans' Administration, the California prison system, and government-funded vocational rehabilitation programs, but the committee disbanded around 1983. Transgender-related policy and legislative accomplishments were few and far between before the early 1990s.

A few transgender organizations and service agencies had soldiered on through the bleakest stretches of the 1970s and '80s. The oldest ongoing transgender gathering in the nation, Fantasia Fair, first met in Provincetown, Massachusetts, in 1975, under the leadership of Ari Kane, a transgender mental health educator who that same year also founded the Outreach Institute of Gender Studies; the weeklong Fantasia Fair, a retreat initially geared toward male-to-female cross-dressers, has tried with some success to broaden its appeal to transsexuals and FTMs in recent years. Boston's transgender community also spawned the International Foundation for Gender Education (IFGE) in 1987; like Fantasia Fair, it initially focused on the needs and interests of MTF cross-dressers but has aimed for an increasingly general transgender constituency during the course of its existence. IFGE's magazine, *Tapestry*, is still probably the most widely circulated transgender publication in the United States. The Janus Information Facility, which had taken over the education and outreach work of the Erickson Foundation in the mid-1970s, itself ceased operations in the mid-1980s and transferred its mission to two stalwarts of the transgender community, Jude Patton and Joanna Clark, who ran the cryptically named transsexual information clearinghouse J2PC (derived from their initials) in San Juan Capistrano, California. Patton and Clark soon passed the torch to a new organization, AEGIS (American Educational Gender Information Service), run by Dallas Denny from her home in rural Georgia. Such small-scale, self-financed, homegrown resources characterized the bulk of what passed for transgender community organizations before the 1990s.

But just as transgender social justice activism made gains in the 1960s, when transgender issues resonated with larger cultural shifts related to the rise of feminism, the war in Vietnam, sexual liberation, and youth countercultures, the transgender movement bolted forward again in the early 1990s for reasons having little to do directly with transgenderism. As suggested earlier, a variety of novel historical factors—the new political concept of queerness, the AIDS epidemic, the rapid development of the Internet, the end of the Cold War, the maturation of the first post–Baby Boom generation, and the turn of the millennium—all played their parts in revitalizing transgender politics in the last decade of the twentieth century. The wave of change that began at that time has not yet reached its crest.

The New Transgender and Feminist Theory

Around 1990, the transgender community experienced a rapid evolution and expansion—indeed, it's about this time that the word "transgender" first started to acquire its current definition as a catchall term for all nonnormative forms of gender expression and identity. Variants of the word had been popping up in male cross-dresser and transvestite communities since the late 1960s, when words such as "transgenderal," "transgenderist," and "transgenderism" were used by people such as Ari Kane and Virginia Prince to describe individuals, such as themselves, who occupied a different gender category from either transvestites or transsexuals. They were searching for a word to describe how they permanently changed their social genders without permanently altering their genitals. Throughout the 1970s and '80s, a "transgenderist" was most likely somebody born with a penis who lived socially as a woman. Trans activist Holly Boswell made an important contribution toward the expansion of the term with her 1991 article "The Transgender Alternative," published in the community-based journal *Chrysalis Quarterly*, which claimed "transgender" is a word that "encompasses the whole spectrum" of gender diversity, that lumps together rather than splits apart the many subgroups within a large, heterogeneous set of communities. Leslie Feinberg gave this expansive sense of "transgender" a political charge with hir influential 1992 pamphlet *Transgender Liberation: A Movement Whose Time Has Come.* Feinberg, who had begun transitioning from female to male in the 1980s before deciding to live again as a masculine woman with some surgical body alterations, became one of the chief architects of the new transgender sensibility, as s/he struggled to define and occupy a space on the borders and intersections of conventional gender categories. Hir pamphlet took a socialist approach to the question of the social, political, and economic oppression of nonnormative expressions of gender, and s/he called for a "transgender" movement that would link many struggles against specific gender-based oppressions together into one radical movement. The following year, Feinberg's semiautobiographical novel *Stone Butch Blues* (1991) communicated the emotional flavor of hir transgender vision to a large and appreciative international audience.

Yet another contribution to the redefinition of "transgender" came in the form of a 1992 academic article by Sandy Stone—"The 'Empire' Strikes Back: A Posttranssexual Manifesto." Stone, who had first gained notoriety in transgender circles as the male-to-female transsexual recording engineer who inspired Janice Raymond to lead a boycott of the all-women Olivia Records collective, had since gotten a PhD in cultural studies, and she made brilliant use of some of the new theories of gender just then beginning to circulate in the academy—which she used to move the old feminist debates about transgenderism into a productive new register. In calling for "posttranssexual" theorizing capable of reframing the common narratives through which trans people were dismissed as either bad, sick, or wrong, Stone helped give the nascent "transgender" movement an intellectual as well as a political agenda.

There is more than one intellectual genealogy of what came to be called "queer studies." One story has it emerging from the work of literary critics Eve Kosofsky Sedgwick and Michael Moon at Duke University. Stone, however, was more grounded in the version of queer feminism that blossomed in Santa Cruz, where she earned her PhD at the University of California while studying under feminist science studies scholar Donna Haraway. West Coast queer theory was more indebted to feminists of color, primarily the writers in the anthology *This Bridge Called My Back,* and most especially to Gloria Anzaldúa's *Borderlands/La Frontera: The New Mestiza.* Two crucial insights in this body of work were to be found in its "intersectional" analyses of race/class/gender/sexuality oppressions—no one of which could be privileged over the others in the lives of the women writing about their situations—and in its attention to "hybridity." White feminism often (and often unconsciously) claimed its moral strength based on some concept of "purity"—notably (especially in the first wave), some notion of female sexual purity, but also, more abstractly, on the idea of an essential womanhood to be recovered or restored from the taint of patriarchal pollution. In contrast, Anzaldúa's brand of feminism valued the power to be found in being mixed, in crossing borders, of having no one clear category to fit into—of being essentially impure. Haraway drew on this evolving frame of reference in her famous essay "A Cyborg Manifesto," which described a "post-gender" world of "technocultural" bodies and added machine/human and animal/human to the kinds of boundary and mixing questions feminism should be concerned with. Stone's "posttranssexual manifesto," concerned as it was with technologically altered transgender bodies, was deeply influenced by Haraway's approach to the intersectionality of gender, embodiment, and technology. However, it also drew from another new way of thinking about gender then being explored by another feminist faculty member at the University of California—Santa Cruz, Teresa de Lauretis, who coined the term "queer studies" for a conference she organized under that name in Santa Cruz in 1991.

The new "queer" version of gender espoused by de Lauretis and other like-minded feminist scholars, which de Lauretis laid out most succinctly in her essay "Technologies of Gender," discarded the older feminist idea that gender was *merely* repressive—that it was *only* a system for holding women down, turning them into second-class citizens, exploiting their labor, and controlling their reproductive capacities. Without denying that gender systems indeed produced systematic inequalities for women, the new queer take on gender also talked about gender's *productive* power—how "woman" was also a "site" or a "location" that its occupants identified themselves with, understood themselves through, and acted from. The new queer feminism drew heavily from French philosopher Michel Foucault's concept of social power as decentralized and distributed rather than flowing from a single source—that is, that each of us has a power particular to our situation,

Transsubjectivity and Reality Hacking

In 1995, I conducted a *Wired* magazine interview with trans theorist Sandy Stone, who has had an amazingly varied career. Among other things, she has done research on digital telephones at Bell Labs, conducted biomedical research on hearing at the Menninger Clinic, worked as sound engineer for Jimi Hendrix, helped found the women's music scene while working at Olivia Records (where she was the target of a transphobic boycott by some lesbian feminists), and earned a PhD in History of Consciousness at the University of California—Santa Cruz. Her article "The 'Empire' Strikes Back: A Posttranssexual Manifesto," a scathing rebuttal to Janice Raymond, helped launch the new interdisciplinary field of transgender studies. Stone now teaches in the Radio, Television, and Film Department at the University of Texas in Austin. Most of what Sandy and I said to each other in that interview for *Wired* wound up on the cutting room floor—here's a version other than the published one, which draws on different parts of our weekend-long conversation.

Stryker: You worked in technical fields for many years but now study how that work is done by others. What led you to cultural studies of science?

Stone: It gave me that common language I'd always dreamed of. I could bring to it much of my experience with neurology and telephony and sound recording and computer programming, my studies of classics, and my brief encounters with critical theory. I could find ways in which all of those things fit together. It started with a piece called "Sex and Death Among the Cyborgs." I set out to write an essay on data compression and wound up writing about phone sex. Sex usually involves as many of the senses as possible—taste, touch, smell, sight, hearing. Phone sex workers translate all those modalities of experience into sound, then boil that down into a series of highly compressed tokens. They squirt those tokens down a voice-grade line and someone at the other end just adds water, so to speak, to reconstitute the tokens into a fully detailed set of images and interactions in multiple sensory modes. "Sex and Death Among the Cyborgs" was an attempt to explore boundaries and prostheses and everything that interests me now.

Stryker: What do you mean when you say "boundaries and prostheses"?

Stone: Subjective boundaries and bodily boundaries. We're a culture that likes to preserve the illusion that they're fixed in place. But they move around all the time. For example, where's the boundary of an individual human body? Is it skin? Is it clothes? It's different in different circumstances. I use Stephen Hawking as an example of how body boundary issues interact with technology. Because Hawking can't speak, he lectures with a computer-generated voice. Hawking's computerized voice generator is a prosthesis, from the Greek word for "extension." It's an extension of his person. It extends his will across the boundaries of flesh and machinery, from the medium of air molecules in motion to the medium of electromagnetic force.

Stryker: It seems to me that being transsexual significantly informs your work. Transsexuality could be considered a form of reality hacking—you "change sex" by using for your own purposes the codes that regulate how we understand the meaning of identity through the body. Hormones and surgery are prostheses that extend a sense of self into a set of physical signs that mean identity in social interactions. Experiencing the transformation of your body through transsexual technologies gives one an acute sense of the issues that come up in trying to understand virtual systems, cyberspace, interface, agency, interaction, and identity. It's hard for many people to grasp this aspect of transsexuality because of the way it's been stigmatized, pathologized, exoticized, and eroticized.

Stone: I want to move away from the sexuality model for very much those reasons—that's why I want to talk about transsubjectivity rather than transsexuality. This term better helps us see that the body is an instrument for involvement with others. When I wrote in an essay called "A Posttranssexual Manifesto" that transsexuality was a genre rather than a gender, I meant that the body is a site for the play of language, a generator of symbolic exchange.

> *Stryker: When we think about consciousness as self-contained and individualistic, bounded by the envelope of our physical bodies instead of being communicative and interactionist, we're still using a seventeenth-century paradigm of subjectivity, one that's in synch with a mechanistic worldview. But we're beginning to see forms of subjectivity that are better modeled by twentieth-century scientific paradigms and their aftermath. One new paradigm I've heard you allude to but not say outright is chaos theory—your idea that it's the turbulence around subjective and bodily boundaries that produces identity.*

> Stone: Now you've picked the right word—"chaos." Identities are in continual flux. They are created interactively in social circumstances. When identity ceases to change, it ceases to exist.

and that power is not just something vested "up there" somewhere in the law or the army or the "patriarchy." Queer feminism reimagined the status "woman" as not simply a condition of victimization to be escaped from, and it reconceived gender as a network of "relations of power" that, like language, we don't ever get outside of but always express ourselves through and work within—a situation that gives feminist women a "dual vision" and "split subjectivity." Sometimes womanhood is a binding-in-place that needs to be resisted and worked against, and sometimes, de Lauretis said, women want womanhood to stick to them "like a wet silk dress."

Without saying so in quite so many words, de Lauretis found a useful way to acknowledge that feminist women could have a nonoppressed gender identity as women while still being committed to feminist politics. This insight in turn opened a line of argument that led directly to Stone's essay, which called upon transsexual people simultaneously to resist the old ways that medical science had encouraged them to behave as the price for providing services—creating false biographies to conceal their sex change from others, for example, or embracing a gender-normative appearance or lifestyle—while also soliciting them to speak out in a "heteroglossic," Babel-like profusion of tongues about all the imaginable genres of gender difference there could be, if only the medically dominated discourse of transsexuality were shattered. In doing so, trans people could simultaneously circumvent older feminist ideas that regarded transsexuals as duplicitous, dupes of the patriarchy, or mentally ill. All genders—all genres of personhood—would be on the same plane.

Two other developments internal to feminism shook open spaces within political activism, scholarship, and community formation that allowed transgender feminism to expand and grow in the 1990s. The first was the so-called "sex wars," a pivotal episode in which was the 1982 Barnard conference on women, which aired long-standing differences within feminism about female sexuality. Fierce debates raged around the topics of pornography, prostitution, and consensual sadomasochism. Could there be feminist positions on these issues that were not simply condemnatory—that is, could there be feminist pornography, feminist sex work, feminist practices of sexual kink, or were such ideas rooted in "internalized misogyny" and did they constitute "violence against women"? The "sex-positive" and "sex-negative" camps were every bit as polarized as those names suggest, and the sex wars—like earlier disputes within feminism about heterosexism, class, and color—further fragmented a movement that was never as homogeneous as some feminists wanted to believe.

Opponents of the "sex-positive" camp consigned cross-dressing and transsexual genital modification to the same discreditable territory occupied by fetish, prostitution, incest, and rape, while the "sex-positive" camp resisted the idea that some sexual practices condemned by mainstream society were intrinsically antifeminist or that criticizing some aspects of those practices necessarily entailed a condemnation of the women who practiced them. The warring perspectives are succinctly summarized in the names of two feminist publications: *Off Our Backs*, which advocated a resistance to sexist oppression of women, and *On Our Backs*, a frank celebration of female sexual pleasure. Some of the same arguments that the sex-positive feminists made in defense of women who take money in exchange for sex or who engage in bedroom bondage scenarios or rape fantasies or intergenerational desire would open a path whereby transgender practices and perspectives could similarly escape the certain promise of feminist censure.

Sex-positive feminism had the disadvantage, however, of regarding trans as an erotic practice rather than an expression of gender identity. Feminist anthropologist Gayle Rubin's influential article "Thinking Sex," first delivered at the Barnard conference and published in the anthology of conference-related work, *Pleasure and Danger,* clearly demonstrates this point. In charting out the "moral sex hierarchy" shared by "sex-negative" feminism and mainstream American society, Rubin distinguishes between forms of sexuality clearly labeled "good" (such as reproductive heterosexual monogamy) and those clearly labeled "bad" (such as fetishistic cross-dressing, transsexuality, or street prostitution), and she identifies a "major area of contest" between these poles that encompasses sexual practices that are morally ambiguous within the dominant culture (such as promiscuous heterosexuality or long-term, stable, romantic homosexual couplings). Through time, a practice might move from a very marginalized position, to one where its status was contested, to one where it was accepted—exactly the path followed by homosexuality in the aftermath of the gay liberation movement.

One of the main goals of Rubin's argument was to challenge the way that some schools of feminism (those drawing on the "purity" tradition) set up hierarchies that placed their own perspective at the top and claimed the power to judge and condemn other positions they deemed morally suspect. Rubin's article most famously noted how early second wave feminism floundered when it tried to apply the economic concept of "class" to the category "woman," which has many noneconomic attributes, and succeeded only when it developed a set of analytical tools that were specific to the situation of women—that is to say, a gender analysis. She then proposed that feminism, as the study of gender, was in turn not a sufficient frame of reference for the analysis of sexuality, and she proposed a new "sexuality studies" that, without abandoning feminism any more than feminism had abandoned economic concerns, would take up a new set of questions about sex. This argument eventually came to be seen as foundational to the intellectual project of queer studies. In making that important argument, however, Rubin clearly categorized transgender practices as sexual or erotic acts rather than expressions of gender identity or sense of self. As the transgender movement began to regather force in the early 1990s, it posed a challenge to the new queer theory similar to the one posed by sexuality to feminism—it asked whether the framework of queer sexuality could adequately account for transgender phenomena, or whether a new frame of analysis was required. These are the questions that led, in the years ahead, to the development of the new interdisciplinary academic field of transgender studies.

Finally, no account of the new transgender movement and its relation to feminism in the early 1990s would be complete without mentioning the impact of philosopher Judith Butler's work. In her 1990 book, *Gender Trouble: Feminism and the Subversion of Identity,* Butler promoted the concept of "gender performativity," which became central to the self-understandings of many transgender people. The main idea is that "being something" consists of "doing it," a point often misunderstood in some quarters of the transgender community as an assertion that gender is a merely a performance and therefore not real. For trans people, who often suffered a great deal to actualize for others the reality of their gender identities, the idea that gender was just a game of sorts, with a wardrobe full of possible gender costumes to be put on or taken off at will, felt galling. But that actually was never Butler's point; rather, it was that the reality of gender for *everybody* is the "doing of it." Rather than being an objective quality of the body (defined by sex), gender is constituted by all the innumerable acts of performing it: how we dress, move, speak, touch, look. Gender is like a language we use to communicate ourselves to others and to understand ourselves. The implication of this argument is that transgender genders are as real as any others, and they are achieved in the same fundamental way.

Butler clarified and extended some of her arguments in her next book, *Bodies That Matter: On the Discursive Limits of "Sex."* She argued there that the category of sex, which is conventionally considered the physical foundation of gender difference (that is, male and female biology respectively generate the social roles and personal identities "man" and "woman"), is actually produced by how culture understands gender. The way a gender system points to the body as a form of evidence that proves its truth is just a discourse, a story we tell about what the evidence of the body means. This discursive truth achieves its reality by being perpetually "cited" (referred to over and over again in medicine, law, psychiatry, media, everyday conversation, and so forth) in ways that, taken all together, effectively make it real—in the performative sense mentioned above. This way of thinking about sex, gender, and reality opened up for theorists within the new transgender movement the prospect that new "truths" of transgender experience, new ways of narrating the relationship between gendered sense of self, social role, and embodiment, could begin to be told—precisely what Sandy Stone had called for in her "posttranssexual" manifesto.

AIDS and the "New Transgender"

The shifting paradigms of gender and sexuality that emerged from the intellectual workplaces of academe by the 1990s were informed by the course of the AIDS epidemic since the 1980s—which also played a vital role in revitalizing the transgender movement. From a public health perspective, transgender populations had come to be seen as "vulnerable" populations—ones more prone to infection (because of the confluence of poverty, social stigma, job discrimination, survival prostitution, fewer educational resources, lack of access to medical information or healthcare, and other contributing factors) To prevent vulnerable populations from becoming vectors of infection for other, larger, populations, AIDS funding entities directed money to "culturally competent" prevention and harm-reduction strategies aimed at trans people. AIDS funding thus became an important mechanism for bringing needed social and financial resources to trans communities. Particularly in communities of color, AIDS agencies and service organizations became centers of transgender activism—hosting support groups, facilitating community gatherings, and providing employment to trans people engaged in health outreach and peer support work. Even strictly social events for trans people who were not HIV-positive were sometimes financially supported through AIDS funding, with the idea that such events could help provide important safer-sex education opportunities and could help build self-esteem and cultural pride that would encourage healthy decision making about potentially risky behaviors. Several organizations and programs established in San Francisco in the early to mid-1990s reflected this national trend, including Projecto ContraSIDA por Vida, the Asian and Pacific Islander Wellness Center, and the transgender program at the Brothers Network, an agency

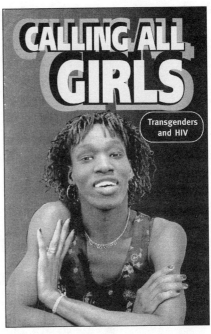

AIDS prevention and educational outreach funding accelerated transgender community formation, especially in communities of color.

primarily serving African American men and transgender women.

The history of the AIDS epidemic significantly reshaped sexual identity politics. When the epidemic first emerged in the United States, it surfaced among gay men who were mostly white. One early name for the syndrome was in fact GRID—Gay-Related Immune Deficiency. But epidemiologists and public health workers knew that the mysterious new disease was not confined to white gay populations and, however much it affected them, to paint the immune deficiency syndrome as "gay related" could serve only to impede an adequate public health response. AIDS also affected hemophiliacs, injection drug users, and Haitian immigrants in disproportionate numbers, regardless of their sexual orientation or gender; it soon became clear that AIDS could pass from person to person through heterosexual intercourse—and that in fact it was the exchange of bodily fluids, rather than sexuality per se, that created risk of infection. The AIDS health crisis thus required gay men, and many lesbians, to rethink the cultural politics of homosexuality and the ways in which homosexual communities related to and intersected with broader social structures—in the same way that it required many nonhomosexuals to relate differently to gay communities and subcultures. To adequately respond to the AIDS epidemic demanded a new kind of alliance politics, in which specific communities came together across the dividing lines of race and gender, class and nationality, citizenship and sexual orientation.

The name for this new kind of unabashedly progay, nonseparatist, antiassimilationist alliance politics to combat AIDS, which did not organize itself around identity categories but instead took aim at the overarching social structures that marginalized the disease and its victims, was *queer*. The new politics resonated with the new intellectual paradigms taking shape in the academy, but it drew its forces from unapologetic, confrontational, and media-savvy protest groups such as ACT-UP (AIDS Coalition to Unleash Power), which reclaimed an old epithet for gay people, "queer," and turned it into an in-your-face "So what?" retort to anti-AIDS prejudice. This newly politicized sense of "queer" first appeared on flyers handed out by militant AIDS organizations at New York's Gay Pride march in June 1990, emblazoned with the headline QUEERS READ THIS! and urging "an army of lovers" to take to the streets. Within days, and for many months, autonomous "Queer Nation" chapters started springing up in cities all across the United States, just as had happened with the Gay Liberation Front in the 1960s. In the two short years that encompassed its waxing and waning, 1990–92, Queer Nation transformed public perceptions of AIDS and homosexuality and shifted internal gay, lesbian, and bisexual community politics in ways that allowed transgender issues to come back into the community's dialogue—just as transgender issues were simultaneously reentering feminism with a new voice.

LGBT (and Sometimes I)

The most direct link between the new queer politics and the transgender movement was the formation in 1992 of Transgender Nation, organized by Anne Ogborn as a focus group within the San Francisco chapter of Queer Nation. QN-SF was a "group of groups" that met monthly so that members of its constituent groups could share ideas, publicize activities, and gather support from other groups for their own actions. Individual groups within QN varied from the women's focus group LABIA (Lesbians and Bisexuals in Action) to SHOP (Suburban Homosexual Outreach Project), and actions varied from staging queer kiss-ins at shopping malls to playing a lead role in massive demonstrations against the Gulf War. If there was an underlying unity to QN's disparate action strategies, it was to be found in the sense of urgency driven by the AIDS crisis and in the conviction that queer people needed to engage immediately in practices that would disrupt the smooth functioning of the heterosexist state. One strategy was simply to erupt into visibility in the everyday spaces of daily city life by how one dressed. Typical QN styles included (then shocking, now mainstream) black leather biker jackets, Doc Martens boots, T-shirts with provocative or cryptic political messages printed on them, tattoos, facial piercings—and copious amounts of Day Glo–colored stickers plastered on any available surface (including the backs of black leather biker jackets), with slogans such as WE ARE EVERYWHERE and WE'RE HERE, WE'RE QUEER, GET USED TO IT. Anne Ogborn had seen a Queer Nation member at a large public protest wearing another popular sticker—TRANS POWER, BI POWER, QUEER NATION—with the words TRANS POWER torn off. She asked the woman wearing the sticker if those words were missing accidentally or on purpose and was told that they had been deliberately removed, because the wearer didn't consider trans people to be part of the queer movement. Ogborn went to the next monthly QN meeting to protest transphobia within the group, and, in typical QN fashion, was invited to organize a focus group devoted to transgender issues.

The announcement in San Francisco's queer press of Transgender

Nation's formation set off a firestorm of protest in the editorial pages—with some of the same lesbian feminists who had attacked Beth Elliott at the West Coast Lesbian Feminist Conference nearly twenty years earlier reviving the same old transphobic rhetoric. This time, however, the communitywide conversation played out differently. A new generation of post–Baby Boomers was reaching adulthood, one whose political sensibilities had been formed by the feminist sex wars, the AIDS crisis, and emerging theoretical perspectives on the sex/gender relationship. Many people who embraced the queer vision of the early 1990s readily accepted transgender as part of the "antiheteronormative" mix. Of course, not all self-identified queers were trans inclusive, nor were all transgender people queer friendly. But a large and previously nonexistent area of overlap between transgender and queer community formations quickly emerged. Transgender Nation erupted with a bang in late 1992, just as QN was falling apart. It initially drew scores of people to its meetings, although it quickly dwindled to a small core of regulars. During its brief existence, its members staged an attention-grabbing protest at the 1993 annual meeting of the American Psychiatric Association that landed three activists in jail; provided courtroom support for transgender women arrested on sex work charges; inspired the formation of a few Transgender Nation chapters in other cities; informed the political sensibilities of an early transgender studies article on "transgender rage"; and made the rounds of LGB groups in San Francisco, demanding that they take a stand on transgender inclusion (thereby demonstrating whether those groups were part of the new queer movement or the old gay and lesbian movement).

During the next few years, members of variously constituted queer groups and organizations in cities across the United States replicated those lively and sometimes heated debates about the relationship between transgender and lesbian, gay, and bisexual communities. The 1993 March on Washington for Lesbian, Gay, and Bi Equal Rights became a particular flashpoint for trans-inclusion struggles after some local organizing committees voted to add "transgender" to the title of the march, but a trans-inclusion resolution failed to pass at the national organizing committee level. Members of Transgender Nation who thereafter showed up in Washington DC to protest the march introduced their new hybrid style of in-your-face queer/transgender politics to transgender and homosexual communities alike—and in doing so helped accelerate subsequent transgender organizing nationwide. By 1994, transgender people played a much larger role in the twenty-fifth anniversary commemoration of the Stonewall Riots, although they were still relegated to the "alternative" march and rally rather than the "official" one. By 1995, however, many formerly "gay and lesbian" or "gay, lesbian, and bisexual" organizations and events were beginning to add the "T" to their names.

This shift in nomenclature toward an "LGBT" community, rather than a "queer" one, marked the beginning of a new phase in the social history of sexual and gender identity politics in the United States. It represented a retreat from the more radical concept of alliance, resistance, and rebellion by different groups against the same oppressive structures in the dominant culture and the adoption instead of a liberal model of minority tolerance and inclusion—sometimes amounting to little more than a "politically correct" gesture of token inclusion for transgender people. While some "LGBT" organizations genuinely addressed transgender concerns in addition to those of sexual orientation minorities, efforts at transgender inclusion often represented a failure to grasp the ways in which transgender identity differed from sexual orientation as well as a misconception about how they were alike.

Most transgender advocates used the word "transgender" as an adjective to describe a way of being a man or a woman or as a way of resisting categorization by those labels. Like class or race or physical ability, "transgender" functioned for them as a descriptive term that cut across the sexual orientation categories, rather than as a noun describing a separate "species" of sexual identity. A transgender man could be gay or straight or bi, in other words, just as he could be black or poor or disabled. Many nontransgendered gays and lesbians, however, regarded the "T" precisely as a new species of sexual identity appended to their own communities. They considered trans people to be, first and foremost, trans people, rather than members of the L, G, or B groups who also just happened to be trans. This misconstruction of transgender identity as a noun rather than an adjective—as a kind of person rather than a descriptive quality—had the unfortunate effect of reinforcing the idea that homosexuality and bisexuality were by definition "gender normative," and that anyone who deviated from the conventional definitions of "man" and "woman" automatically belonged in the transgender category. This way of thinking about transgender tended to reinforce the similarities between homosexual cultures and mainstream society based on shared concepts of gender and to perpetuate the marginalization of transgender people, both within mainstream society and the LGBT movement.

One other related development in the early 1990s that deserves attention is the emergence of an intersex political movement. Cheryl Chase founded the Intersex Society of North America (ISNA) in San Francisco in 1993 with the single-minded goal of ending the practice of pediatric genital surgeries on babies born with ambiguous genitalia (clearly neither male or female)—as Chase herself had been. Chase had been assigned male at birth, but, a few years later, doctors reversed their decision, told her parents to raise her as a girl, and performed surgery to reduce what they had formerly considered a very small penis to an "appropriate" size for what they now considered a clitoris (and thus too big). Chase did not remember her early childhood gender reassignment, which is exactly what the medical professionals thought best in terms of helping intersex kids to develop a "normal" gender. But rather than helping Chase feel "normal," the nonconsensual genital surgeries, which severely compromised her ability to have an orgasm later in life, left her feeling like a sexually dysfunctional freak. When she discovered as an adult what had happened to her as a child, which had deliberately been kept secret from her, Chase felt as if her entire life had been built on a lie. Nothing had prepared her to accept either her hermaphroditic body or the surgeries that tried in vain to normalize it. After briefly contemplating suicide, Chase resolved instead that no other children should suffer what she herself had experienced. Chase moved from Japan to San Francisco to learn what she could from the new queer and transgender activism that had erupted there.

The result was ISNA, which has made tremendous progress in changing the way that the medical establishment treats ambiguous genitalia, providing peer support for intersex people and their families, and educating the general public about intersexuality. Chase considered intersex politics to be related to queer and transgender politics not only because they all challenged medical authority and called for the reform of powerful social institutions, but also because the practice of normalizing surgery was such a visceral example of the idea that beliefs about gender actually produced the sex of the body, rather than the other way around. Bodies that did not originally fit the gender binary were literally cut to fit into it, and the process whereby the operation attempted to produce "normal" as a result was rendered invisible, its recipients silenced—just as the medical establishment had attempted to do with transsexuals. ISNA also offered a feminist perspective on intersex surgeries. The vast majority of children with ambiguous genitalia are eventually assigned as female, because surgeons find it far easier to remove "excess" tissue than to build up new body structures for genitals deemed insufficient for a normal male appearance. This fixation on penis size, coupled with a cultural devaluation of the feminine that already conceived of women as "lacking" what men have, conspires to inflict unnecessary surgeries on intersex children. As feminist sociologist Suzanne Kessler noted in her work on the biomedical ethics of intersex surgeries, ambiguous genitalia are rarely dangerous for a baby's health, but they are very dangerous for that baby's culture. Although contemporary intersex and transgender activism sometimes intersect and overlap one another, they have trended in separate directions. They have common roots, however, in the queer politics of the early 1990s.

Forging a National Transgender Community

The transgender community grew in so many different directions during the first half of the 1990s, and from so many different locations, that it's impossible to place all the developments into a single chronological narrative. Gradually, a widely dispersed network of new groups and campaigns began to influence one another, forging a more coherent national perspective. One of the first transgender-related events to break out of local notoriety and into national prominence in the early days of the new transgender movement was the 1991 expulsion of transwoman Nancy Jean Burkholder from the Michigan Womyn's Music Festival. The long-running festival, which combines outdoor camping with several days of musical performances, and which advertises itself as a women-only event, had a tacit, unstated policy of not welcoming transgender women on the grounds that they were not "womyn-born-womyn"—that is, since transwomen did not share the experience of being raised as girls, and had experienced early socialization as boys, they therefore could never really understand what it meant to be a woman under patriarchy or appreciate the need for women-only spaces. Burkholder, who claimed not to have known of the antitranssexual policy, was deeply troubled by her expulsion and began speaking out in queer and transgender publications. Her case quickly came to function as a litmus test for whether "queer" was indeed transgender inclusive. In subsequent years, transgender activists and allies have organized a "Camp Trans" near the music festival grounds to offer ongoing protest, educational outreach, dialogue, alternative community formations, and networking opportunities to combat transphobia. The debates about transgender participation at the Michigan Womyn's Music Festival remain an important touchstone in continually evolving queer, transgender, and feminist political discussions.

Another milestone in 1991 was the first Southern Comfort transgender conference in Atlanta—a large-scale version of the same sorts of activities that have long characterized local transgender group meetings: guest speakers, workshops, discussions, entertainment, and socializing. Through the years, that event has grown into one of the largest regular transgender gatherings in the country; it provided the setting for the award-winning 2001 documentary film *Southern Comfort,* which chronicled the final years in the life of transman Robert Eads, a conference regular, who died of ovarian cancer after being unable to get healthcare because of his transgender status. In 1992 in Houston, longtime transgender activist and attorney Phyllis Frye organized the first of six annual transgender law conferences, formally titled the International Conference on Transgender Law and Employment Policy. The published proceedings of the conference did much to inspire a new burst of transgender legal activism and to connect activists at the national level. Frye was also instrumental in orchestrating a transgender contingent at the 1993 LGB March on Washington and in beginning to lobby federal legislators on transgender legal and policy issues—everything from healthcare coverage for transgender medical procedures to rules governing state-issued IDs, to employment nondiscrimination protection to hate crimes legislation. Maryland's Jessica Xavier, who served on the local host committee for the 1993 march, also took an active role in transgender political lobbying in the early 1990s, founding both the Washington DC chapter of Transgender Nation and organizing another national transgender political lobbying group, It's Time America. Another trans activist from the nation's capital, Martine Rothblatt, drew parallels between race-based and transgender oppressions with her 1996 book, *The Apartheid of Sex*.

In New York, activist Riki Wilchins cited lesbian and feminist history—specifically the Lavender Menace and Radicalesbians—when she launched the Transexual Menace in 1994, whose trademark image was a Goth-styled black T-shirt emblazoned with the group's name in blood-dripping red letters. Wilchins and the Transexual Menace garnered unprecedented media attention by sponsoring vigils outside of courthouses where cases involving antitransgender crimes were being tried (notably the 1993 rape and murder of Brandon Teena in Nebraska), and they became the subject of iconic gay liberation filmmaker Rosa Von Praunheim's 1996 documentary *Transexual Menace*. Wilchins went on to found the Gender Public Advocacy Coalition (GenderPAC), one of the better-funded national organizations working on gender rights. She also expanded transgender lobbying efforts on Capitol Hill and wrote an acerbic primer on her version of the new transgender politics, *Read My Lips: Sexual Subversion and the End of Gender*.

In San Francisco, Kiki Whitlock and other transgender activists worked

Remembering Our Dead

Transgender people, as a group, experience one of the highest rates of violence and murder in the United States. During the course of the 1990s, several high-profile homicides gave the transgender social justice movement a heightened sense of urgency.

One of the most notorious incidents took place outside Falls City, Nebraska, on December 31, 1993, during the first flush of the new wave of transgender activism, when John Lotter and Tom Nissen murdered a female-bodied individual who was just beginning to live as a young man who went by "Brandon" (among several other names). Brandon, who was christened Teena Brandon at birth, gained posthumous celebrity as Brandon Teena through his tragic murder; he has been the subject of several mass media projects, including Aphrodite Jones's sensationalistic true crime paperback *All She Wanted*, the Guggenheim-commissioned online multimedia installation *Brandon*, the documentary film *The Brandon Teena Story*, and the feature film *Boys Don't Cry*, for which then-newcomer Hilary Swank won the Academy Award for Best Actress for her portrayal of Brandon.

Brandon, originally from Omaha but trying to escape an unhappy home life, had drifted to rural Falls City. There he began dating a young woman who claimed initially not to know that he was biologically female, and he was befriended by Lotter and Nissen. Upon the revelation of Brandon's anatomical sex, his supposed friends raped him; Brandon reported the rape to the county sheriff, who took no action. A few days later Nissen and Lotter tracked Brandon down at another friend's rented farmhouse, where early on the morning of New Year's Eve they shot and killed him and two other young people staying in the house. The two killers were eventually convicted of homicide; Lotter received a death sentence and Nissen life imprisonment without possibility of parole.

with the city's Human Rights Commission in 1993 and 1994 to produce a landmark report, principally written by FTM community leader Jamison Green, that documented human rights abuses against the transgender community at an unprecedented level of detail. That report became the basis for San Francisco's 1995 transgender antidiscrimination ordinance, one of several such local measures passed nationwide in the mid-1990s.

THE CURRENT WAVE 143

Because Brandon had lived for only a short while as a man, had expressed to some people his desire to transition from female to male but had not yet begun hormone treatment, surgical body alterations, or legal change of name and gender, and offered several (sometimes conflicting) accounts of his identity, sexuality, and plans for future life, his story became a flashpoint in identity skirmishes in the GLBT community. Some members of the lesbian and gay community considered Brandon a butch lesbian, while some members of the transgender community saw that claim as an affront to his transmasculinity. The important point recognized by most everyone, however, was the extent to which the lack of congruence between Brandon's pronouns and genitals became the target of a deadly transphobic, homophobic, and misogynistic rage.

Transgender activists organized by Riki Wilchins held vigils outside the courthouse in Falls Creek during the trial for Brandon's murder. For several years thereafter, activists continued to hold vigils whenever possible in other cases of violence against transgender people to draw media attention to this chronic but underreported problem.

The most recent highly publicized murder of a transgender person involved Gwen Araujo, a California teenager who was beaten and strangled to death in 2002 by several male acquaintances, with some of whom she reportedly had been sexually active, after she was discovered to have male genitalia. Defense lawyers attempted to use the so-called "panic defense," in which heterosexual defendants in antigay and antitransgender murder or assault cases claim their actions are justified because of the panic they experience when confronted with the possibility of committing an act they consider "homosexual." That argument was not successful, however, with the Araujo case jury, which returned guilty verdicts for the assailants. Many transgender activists consider the weakening of the panic defense to be one of the few positive results of the case. A Lifetime cable network movie about the case, *A Girl Like Me: The Gwen Araujo Story*, aired on June 19, 2006.

In the decade ahead, San Francisco built upon this foundation to begin offering its transgender citizens greater and greater legal protections against discrimination—and even offered transgender city employees healthcare benefits that covered the cost of their gender transitions.

Along with political activism, transgender cultural production picked up pace in the early 1990s. Academic work reflecting the new transgender perspectives and political sensibilities began appearing in peer-reviewed professional journals, and many of the new breed of transgender scholars—many of them struggling to break into the ranks of tenured professorships but finding in academe the same kinds of employment discrimination that transgender people faced everywhere—first met face to face at the 1994 Iowa Queer Studies Conference. The next year, the highly regarded historian of sexuality Vern Bullough organized the First International Conference on Cross-Dressing, Sex, and Gender at California State University at Northridge, which brought the new wave of transgender scholarship into face-to-face engagement with old-school researchers. Subsequent gatherings (which eventually started describing themselves as "transgender studies conferences") were held in Philadelphia, Oxford (U.K.), Perth (Australia), and other cities around the world. Before the end of the decade, the prestigious *Chronicle of Higher Education* had published a feature article recognizing the emergence of transgender studies as a new interdisciplinary field; transgender-related material was being integrated into college courses in a wide range of disciplines, and a steady stream of transgender scholarship was rolling off the press.

In the arts, playwright and actor Kate Bornstein prodded audiences from coast to coast to think about gender in new ways with her stage shows *Hidden: A Gender* and *Strangers in Paradox,* and her 1995 book, *Gender Outlaw: On Men, Women, and the Rest of Us*—all of which helped to define transgender style in the 1990s. David Harrison, another playwright and actor, chronicled female-to-male experience in his popular performance-festival-circuit crowd-pleaser, *FTM.* The first FTM Conference of the Americas was held in San Francisco in 1995 (ironically, at the San Francisco Women's Building, which rents its meeting spaces to a wide variety of progressive causes). Transmen soon received even more exposure through photographer Loren Cameron's portraiture work, collected in the 1996 volume *Body Alchemy,* which included a stunning self-portrait, *God's Will,* showing Cameron's own gym-sculpted and testosterone-enhanced physique, a remote camera-shutter release clutched in one hand, a syringe in the other, and the artist fully in control of both self-image and the image-making process. Another photographer, Mariette Pathy Allen, who had been documenting the male-to-female cross-dresser and transgender community since the early 1980s, and who has since gone on to document transgender youth and gender-variant practices in Asia and the Pacific Islands, also began to document the flourishing FTM scene in the mid-1990s.

Mainstream media began paying heightened attention to transgender themes with the 1992 box-office smash *The Crying Game,* whose onscreen story, revolving around the gender ambiguity of the lead character, Dil, was echoed by offscreen speculations about the actual gender of the film's star, Jaye Davidson. Major stories on the new transgender scene started appearing in high-profile publications such as the *New Yorker,* the *New York Times,* and *Mother Jones.* Subcultural outlets for transgender culture erupted at the same time in a spate of new, low-budget, do-it-yourself zine publications, including Kansas City's *TransSisters: The Journal of Transsexual Feminism,* San Francisco's *TNT: The Transsexual News Telegraph,* and Toronto's *Gendertrash.* These publications continued a tradition of small-scale transgender community publishing that stretched back to Virginia Prince's first *Transvestia* magazine in 1952. Several of them, particularly *Gendertrash,* drew inspiration from the still-flourishing punk zine culture of the later 1970s and 1980s and formed part of the larger subcultural phenomenon sometimes called the "queer zine explosion," a

Loren Cameron's Body Alchemy *was a prominent part of the new wave of visibility for transgender men in the 1990s.*

remarkable outpouring of self-published, sometimes highly ephemeral, periodical publications about art, culture, and politics that constituted an important facet of the broader queer movement.

The first half of the 1990s represented a high-water mark in the tradition of such publications, the numbers and frequency of which dropped off precipitously in the middle of the decade, in reverse proportion to the rise of the Internet age. Although the Internet had been around for a long time by then, its use had been mostly confined to scientists and computer geeks, and largely limited to email and electronic bulletin boards, until Netscape introduced Navigator, the first user-friendly web browser, in 1996. Almost overnight, the Internet became a cheaper distribution outlet than even the cheapest paper-based, surface-mailed publications—and, once the first generation of search engines made finding online content as easy as typing a search term, one capable of reaching vast potential audiences. The Internet had more important consequences for the transgender movement, however, than killing off its zines. As was true for other groups that experienced high degrees of social isolation, or were spread out over large geographical areas, the Internet helped connect transgender people who otherwise might not have been in touch with one another. The remarkable expansion of the transgender movement in the mid-1990s would not have been possible without the Internet's even more remarkable and rapid transformation of the means of mass communication.

The new burst of transgender activism in the 1990s was framed, from beginning to end, by larger historical narratives. The Cold War, which had polarized the globe since World War II, had come to an end with the fall of the Berlin Wall in 1988 and the collapse of the Soviet Union in 1992, and many residents of the West were absolutely giddy with the prospect of what then-president George H. W. Bush called a "New World Order" to be dominated by the interests of the United States, the sole remaining global superpower. With the new millennium looming just a few years in the future, the stock market racing to unheard-of heights in the speculative frenzy of the dot-com boom, and with technology transforming everyday life in unprecedented ways, transgender issues—which seemed to unhinge familiar reality by breaking the accustomed bonds between bodily sex and gendered appearance—came to be seen as harbingers of the strange new world beginning to take shape. This moment of premillennial fantasy was captured as it happened in experimental filmmaker Monika Treut's 1999 *Gendernauts,* which cast transgender people as bold adventurers setting out into the uncharted territory of humanity's technologically and biomedically enhanced future.

Twenty-First-Century Transformations

Twenty-first-century transgender reality is of course proving to be far more mundane and more or less a continuation and consolidation of the trends of the preceding several years. Transmen continued to gain in visibility, to the point that many younger people (especially those enrolled in traditionally women-only colleges) now associate "transgender" more readily with female-bodied masculinity than they do with male-to-female individuals—particularly given the appearance of long-awaited major nonfiction books by FTM authors Jamison Green *(Becoming a Visible Man)* and Max Wolf Valerio *(The Testosterone Files)* and rising-star performers such as Imani Henry, dancer Sean Dorsey, and hip-hop artist Katastrophe. Transgender mass media representation is both more frequent and less prejudicial, with cable shows such as *TransGenerations,* the feature film *TransAmerica,* and the stage and screen extravaganzas *Hedwig and the Angry Inch* finding large and appreciative audiences. Musical performers such as Antony Hegarty, lead singer of the performance ensemble Antony and the Johnsons (named in honor of transgender hero Marsha P. Johnson) push transgender style in unanticipated new artistic directions. A genderqueer denizen of New York nightclubs in the 1990s, Antony's emotive vocal style and poignant lyrics express the power and pathos of living outside the gender binary. Antony's art—which broke out of the underground club scene thanks to the patronage of perennially cutting-edge artists Lou Reed and Laurie Anderson—links transgender sensibilities to the cultural avant-garde in ways not seen since the 1960s. A spate of new authors in the transgender

Antony Hegarty of the ensemble Antony and the Johnsons (named for transgender pioneer Marsha P. Johnson) infuses a transgender sensibility into the avant-garde group's musical performances.

community include memoirists Jennifer Boylan, author of *She's Not There* (and a frequent guest on Oprah Winfrey's talk show), and Helen Boyd, author of *My Husband Betty* and *She's Not the Man I Married*, as well as transfeminist writer Julia Serano and the contributors to Mattilda's (aka Matt Bernstein Sycamore's) anthology *Nobody Passes*.

On the Internet, Gwen Smith's Remembering Our Dead website, launched in 1999, put a spotlight on the chronic undercurrent of antitransgender violence that leaves, on average, one transgender person dead from hate crimes every month. A related commemoration of the year's dead, Transgender Day of Remembrance, is now observed on high school and college campuses and community centers around the world, and it has become an annual opportunity to publicize the persistence of antitransgender prejudice and violence in spite of recent civil rights gains. At the outset of the 1990s, only three municipalities in the country offered any kind of legal protection for transgender people living and working in their jurisdictions, and only one state, Minnesota, offered protections at the state level, beginning in 1993. By the time the new century began, there were twenty-six localities with some form of transgender protection; as of 2007, there were more than a hundred, in addition to thirteen states and the District of Columbia. That year, the first piece of federal legislation ever to address transgender concerns, a hate crimes bill, passed both the Senate and House of Representatives.

A great deal of credit for twenty-first-century legislative victories is due to a new crop of legal activist organizations, including the Sylvia Rivera Law Project in New York; the Transgender Law Center

Transgender Rights

Human Rights Laws in the United States That Explicitly Include Transgendered People*

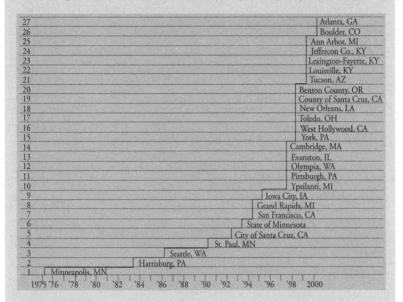

27	Atlanta, GA
26	Boulder, CO
25	Ann Arbor, MI
24	Jeffercon Co., KY
23	Lexington-Fayette, KY
22	Louisville, KY
21	Tucson, AZ
20	Benton County, OR
19	County of Santa Cruz, CA
18	New Orleans, LA
17	Toledo, OH
16	West Hollywood, CA
15	York, PA
14	Cambridge, MA
13	Evanston, IL
12	Olympia, WA
11	Pittsburgh, PA
10	Ypsilanti, MI
9	Iowa City, IA
8	Grand Rapids, MI
7	San Francisco, CA
6	State of Minnesota
5	City of Santa Cruz, CA
4	St. Paul, MN
3	Seattle, WA
2	Harrisburg, PA
1	Minneapolis, MN

1975 '76 '78 '80 '82 '84 '86 '88 '90 '92 '94 '96 '98 2000

*Years indicate the date the law was passed, not the date the law was put into effect. This chart does not include jurisdictions such as Washington, DC, that have case law interpreting the "personal appearance" category as covering transgendered people. See District of Columbia, Human Rights Act of 1977, Title I, Chapter 25, Sec. 1–2502, (22).

Reprinted from Paisley Currah and Shannon Minter, Transgender Equality: A Handbook for Activists and Policymakers (Washington, DC: National Gay and Lesbian Task Force, 2000).

in San Francisco, which began as a project of the National Center for Lesbian Rights; the National Center for Transgender Equality, the lead transgender lobbying organization in Washington DC; and the National Transgender Advocacy Coalition (NTAC), which draws its leadership from nonmetropolitan and noncoastal parts of the country.

Two historically gay organizations, Lambda Legal and the National Gay and Lesbian Task Force, have provided invaluable support for transgender legal campaigns undertaken by community leaders and allies such as Paisley Currah, Shannon Minter, Cecilia Chung, Chris Daley, Monica Roberts, Autumn Sandeen, Marti Abernathy, Dean Spade, Pauline Park, and many others.

As significant as participation in queer and LGBT politics has been for the transgender movement since the early 1990s, events of the early twenty-first century demonstrate how vital it is for transgender activism to think beyond the comparatively narrow scope of sexuality and gender identity politics. Since the terrorist attacks of September 11, 2001, heightened border surveillance, increased attention to travel documents, and more stringent standards for obtaining state-issued identification all have made life more complicated for many transgender people. Depending on variables such as where they happened to be born or what levels of healthcare they can afford, some transgender people find it impossible to obtain tightly controlled identity documents (such as passports) that accurately reflect their current name or gender appearance—which makes travel impossible in some circumstances and risky or dangerous in others. The restrictions on movement in the post-9/11 United States give transgender people more in common with immigrants, refugees, and undocumented workers than they might have with the gay and lesbian community. Pursuing transgender justice increasingly involves joining campaigns and struggles that might seem at first to have little to do with gender identity or expression—but everything to do with how the state polices those who differ from social norms and tries to solve the bureaucratic problems that arise from attempting to administer the lives of atypical members of its population.

A striking example of how transgender interests can diverge from legal activism related to sexual orientation can be found in the debates about transgender inclusion in the federal Employment Non-Discrimination Act, late in 2007. First introduced for consideration by Congresswoman Bella Abzug in the 1970s, ENDA, as the bill is known, aims to prohibit employment discrimination based on sexual orientation. The proposed legislation didn't make it out of committee for a full congressional debate until 1994, when the measure failed to pass by a single vote. At that time, the transgender movement did not have sufficient political clout to have gender identity or gender expression provisions added to the language of the bill—indeed, ENDA's primary lobbyist, the Human Rights Campaign (HRC), actively undermined transgender activists who were just then beginning to lobby Congress for transgender inclusion within the bill. But as the "T" became more and more integrated into the fabric of the LGBT community, major political organizations such as the National Gay and Lesbian Task Force, PFLAG (Parents, Families and Friends of Lesbians and Gays), and other groups began to advocate for transgender inclusion. Over the course of a decade, virtually every national and state organization representing LGBT interests came to support transgender inclusion in federal employment protection legislation. They argued that transgender people were in fact the most severely discriminated against of all the LGBT communities, and that, moreover, most discrimination against gay, lesbian, and bisexual people who were not transgendered was rooted in prejudices about gender-normative appearances and behaviors—that is, it was the too-effeminate gay man, or the too-masculine woman, who was more vulnerable to employment discrimination than straight-looking, straight-acting homosexual men and women. A gradual consensus emerged among those most active in advancing the LGBT legislative agenda that adding employment protections for gender identity and expression was a necessary amendment to ENDA—one that would protect all Americans from being fired for failing to live up to a stereotype of masculine or feminine social roles, and that would be especially beneficial for transgender people in particular.

When Democrats took control of both houses of Congress after the midterm elections in 2006, ENDA was poised for passage for the first time since 1994. In the spring of 2007, even the HRC—long a holdout on a transgender-inclusive legislative strategy—finally got on board and lobbied in support of a version of ENDA that protected gender identity and expression as well as sexual orientation. All seemed to be going well until September 2007, when the bill's longtime sponsor, the openly gay Massachusetts congressman Barney Frank, decided, on the basis of an informal poll of his colleagues, that a sexual-orientation-only version of ENDA could pass, but that a transgender-inclusive version would fail. Rather than wait to gather additional support or conduct more extensive education and lobbying efforts, Frank took it upon himself to split ENDA into two separate bills—one for sexual orientation and the other for gender identity.

The reaction in the LGBT community was swift and unprecedented—more than three hundred national, state, and local organizations formed an ad hoc campaign, United ENDA, to demand that transgender-inclusive language be restored to the bill. LGBT activists all across the country felt that more than a decade's worth of work to build a more expansive movement had been betrayed at the last minute by the movement's congressional leadership. At the same time, many lesbian and gay people who had never felt entirely comfortable being linked to transgender issues since the mid-1990s gave voice to long-suppressed antitransgender attitudes that they'd formerly considered too "politically incorrect" to express publicly—and supported splitting ENDA into two bills. HRC, which had only recently come to support transgender-inclusive language in ENDA, lost what little credibility it had with the transgender community when it made an abrupt about-face and endorsed the sexual-orientation-only version of the bill. In the end, the trans-inclusive version of ENDA died in committee, while the sexual-orientation-only version passed the House of Representatives—a Pyrrhic victory, given that President Bush promised to veto any version of ENDA that made it to his desk.

As a result of the ENDA controversy, the LGBT movement that transgender people have worked to build since the early 1990s may well be split apart by legislative fiat. More than ever, gay and lesbian people who conform to gender norms seem poised for mainstream acceptance, while discrimination against gender-norm transgression remains legal. The old LGBT movement is splintering, and transgender issues are now clearly the cutting edge of the social justice agenda. The growing acceptability of transgender representation in mass media, and the increasing comfort younger people seem to have with transgender and genderqueer identities and behaviors, suggests that sometime in the future—perhaps the near future—transgender people will finally be accepted as full, equal members of society. But much work remains to be done.

READER'S GUIDE

Questions for Discussion

How did this book change your perspective on transgender history?

What do you consider the most important development in the past fifty years for transgender rights? Why?

Name or describe three transgender people you've seen portrayed in the media. How were these individuals depicted? What social values or ideas do you think these depictions reflect?

What issues do you think the transgender movement most urgently needs to work on in your state or city?

What does it mean when an employer agrees to not discriminate against workers or customers based on their gender identity? What sort of actions, policies, or changes do you think this nondiscrimination would involve?

Consider the different approaches that people in the transgender movement have used to effect civic change (street activism, uprisings, marches, letter writing, lobbying, the formation of nonprofit organizations, et cetera). What do you see as the successes and failings of each approach? Do you think any one approach has been more effective than the rest? Explain your answers.

How has attention to transgender issues changed feminism? Do you think third wave feminism differs from second wave feminism regarding its approach to transgender issues? How so?

Topics for Research

Pick one of the following topics and research how the situation in your state has evolved in past decades:

Human Rights

Questions to consider: What sort of legal rights do transgender individuals have in your state or local area? If your state has antidiscrimination laws protecting transgender people, what protections do they afford? How did these laws come about? What groups or individual activists have worked on the issue in your state? Did transgender people and nontransgender people work together on transgender rights issues in your state?

Employment

Questions to consider: In your state or local area, are transgender people legally protected from workplace discrimination? If not, what groups or individuals are working to institute these workplace protections? Have there been any individual or class-action lawsuits in your state to address discrimination? Which employers in your state have policies that prohibit discrimination based on gender identity?

Access to Health Services

Questions to consider: What local health services exist that address transgender people's health needs? When were they established? If you cannot find any such organizations in your state, where is the nearest transgender-friendly health service you can find? How much would it cost to travel there from your city?

Identity

Questions to consider: Are transgender individuals in your state allowed to change their sex on legal documents, such as driver's licenses? If so, when was this right instituted? If not, what groups are working to change the law? What concrete differences does this right make in the lives of transgender people?

FURTHER READING AND RESOURCES

BOOKS: NONFICTION

Atkins, Dawn, ed. *Looking Queer: Body Image and Identity in Lesbian, Bisexual, Gay, and Transgender Communities*. New York: Haworth, 1998.

Bailey, J. Michael. *The Man Who Would Be Queen: The Science of Gender-Bending and Transsexualism*. Washington, DC: Joseph Henry, 2003.

Beam, Cris. *Transparent: Love, Family, and Living the T with Transgender Teens*. New York: Harcourt, 2007.

Benjamin, Harry. *The Transsexual Phenomenon*. New York: Julian, 1966.

Blackwood, Evelyn, and Saskia Wieringa, eds. *Female Desires: Same-Sex Relations and Transsexual Practices Across Cultures*. New York: Columbia University, 1999.

Bloom, Amy. *Normal: Transsexual CEOs, Crossdressing Cops, and Hermaphrodites with Attitude*. New York: Random House, 2002.

Bolin, Anne. *In Search of Eve: Transsexual Rites of Passage*. South Hadley, MA: Bergin and Garvey, 1987.

Bornstein, Kate. *Gender Outlaw: On Men, Women, and the Rest of Us*. New York: Routledge, 1994.

Bullough, Bonnie, ed. *Gender Blending*. Amherst, MA: Prometheus, 1997.

Bullough, Vern, and Bonnie Bullough. *Cross Dressing, Sex, and Gender*. Philadelphia: University of Pennsylvania, 1993.

Butler, Judith. *Bodies That Matter: On the Discursive Limits of Sex*. New York: Routledge, 1993.

———. *Gender Trouble: Feminism and the Subversion of Identity*. New York: Routledge, 1990.

———. *Undoing Gender*. New York: Routledge, 2004.

Califia, Patrick. *Sex Changes: The Politics of Transgenderism*. San Francisco: Cleis, 2003.

Cameron, Loren. *Body Alchemy: Transsexual Portraits*. San Francisco: Cleis, 1996.

Cromwell, Jason. *Transmen and FTMs: Identities, Bodies, Genders, and Sexualities.* Urbana: University of Illinois, 1999.

Currah, Paisley, Richard M. Juang, and Shannon Price Minter, eds. *Transgender Rights.* Minneapolis: University of Minnesota, 2006.

Denny, Dallas, ed. *Current Concepts in Transgender Identity.* New York: Routledge, 1997.

Devor, Holly. *FTM: Female-to-Male Transsexuals in Society.* Bloomington: Indiana University, 1997.

———. *Gender Blending: Confronting the Limits of Duality.* Bloomington: Indiana University, 1989.

Diamond, Morty, ed. *From the Inside Out: Radical Gender Transformation, FTM and Beyond.* San Francisco: Manic D, 2004.

Doctor, Richard. *Transvestites and Transsexuals: Toward a Theory of Cross-Gender Behavior.* New York: Plenum, 1988.

Ekins, Richard. *Male Femaling: A Grounded Theory Approach to Cross-Dressing and Sex-Changing.* New York: Routledge, 1997.

Ekins, Richard, and Dave King. *The Transgender Phenomenon.* London: Sage, 2006.

Epstein, Julia, and Kristina Straub, eds. *Body Guards: The Cultural Politics of Gender Ambiguity.* New York: Routledge, 1991.

Fausto-Sterling, Anne. *Sexing the Body: Gender Politics and the Construction of Sexuality.* New York: Perseus, 1999.

Feinberg, Leslie. *Transgender Warriors: Making History from Joan of Arc to Dennis Rodman.* Boston: Beacon, 1996.

———. *Trans Liberation: Beyond Pink or Blue.* Boston: Beacon, 1998.

Feinbloom, Deborah Heller. *Transvestites and Transsexuals.* New York: A Delta Book, 1976.

Foucault, Michel. *Herculin Barbin: Being the Recently Discovered Memoirs of a Nineteenth-Century Hermaphrodite.* New York: Pantheon, 1980.

———. *The History of Sexuality: An Introduction.* New York: Vintage, 1990. First published 1978.

Friedman, Mack. *Strapped for Cash: A History of American Hustler Culture*, Los Angeles: Alyson, 2003.

Green, Richard, and John Money, eds. *Transsexualism and Sex Reassignment.* Baltimore: Johns Hopkins University, 1969.

Grosz, Elizabeth. *Space, Time, and Perversion: Essays on the Politics of Bodies.* New York: Routledge, 1995.

———. *Volatile Bodies: Toward a Corporeal Feminism.* Bloomington: Indiana University, 1994.

Grosz, Elizabeth, and Elsbeth Probyn, eds. *Sexy Bodies: The Strange Carnalities of Feminism.* New York: Routledge, 1995.

Halberstam, Judith. *Female Masculinity.* Durham, NC: Duke University, 1998.

———. *In a Queer Time and Place: Transgender Bodies, Subcultural Lives.* New York: New York University, 2005.

Halberstam, Judith, and Ira Livingston, eds. *Posthuman Bodies.* Bloomington: Indiana University, 1995.

Hausman, Bernice L. *Changing Sex: Transsexualism, Technology, and the Idea of Gender.* Durham, NC: Duke University, 1995.

Haynes, Felicity, and Tarquam McKenna, eds. *Unseen Genders: Beyond the Binaries.* New York: Peter Lang, 2001.

Irving, Janice. *Disorders of Desire: Sex and Gender in Modern American Sexology.* Philadelphia: Temple University, 1990.

Jacobs, Sue-Ellen, Wesley Thomas, and Sabine Lang, eds. *Two-Spirit People: Native American Gender Identity, Sexuality, and Spirituality.* Urbana: University of Illinois, 1997.

Johnson, Mark. *Beauty and Power: Transgendering and Cultural Transformation in the Southern Philippines.* Oxford: Berg, 1997.

Kane-Demaios, J. Ari, and Vern L. Bullough, eds. *Crossing Sexual Boundaries: Transgender Journeys, Uncharted Paths.* Amherst, MA: Prometheus, 2005.

Kessler, Suzanne J. *Lessons from the Intersexed.* Piscataway, NJ: Rutgers University, 1998.

King, Dave. *The Transvestite and the Transsexual: Public Categories and Private Identities.* Aldershot: Avebury, 1993.

Kotula, Dean. *The Phallus Palace: Female to Male Transsexuals.* Boston: Alyson, 2002.

Kroker, Arthur, and Marlilouise Kroker. *The Last Sex: Feminism and Outlaw Bodies.* New York: St. Martin's, 1993.

Lang, Sabine. *Men as Women, Women as Men: Changing Gender in Native American Cultures.* Austin: University of Texas, 1998.

Laqueur, Thomas. *Making Sex: Body and Gender from the Greeks to Freud.* Cambridge, MA: Harvard University, 1990.

Lothstein, Leslie Martin. *Female-to-Male Transsexualism: Historical, Clinical, and Theoretical Issues.* New York and Boston: Routledge and Kegan Paul, 1983.

MacKenzie, Gordene Olga. *Transgender Nation.* Bowling Green, OH: Bowling Green University, 1994.

Mattilda, a.k.a. Matt Bernstein Sycamore, ed. *Nobody Passes: Rejecting the Rules of Gender and Conformity.* Berkeley, CA: Seal, 2006.

Meyerowitz, Joanne. *How Sex Changed: A History of Transsexuality in the United States.* Cambridge, MA: Harvard University, 2002.

More, Kate, and Stephen Whittle, eds. *Reclaiming Genders: Transsexual Grammars at the Fin de Siècle.* London: Cassell, 1999.

Namaste, Vivian K. *Invisible Lives: The Erasure of Transsexual and Transgendered People.* Chicago: University of Chicago, 2000.

———. *Sex Change, Social Change: Reflections on Identity, Institutions, and Imperialism.* Toronto: Women's Press, 2005.

Nanda, Serena. *Gender Diversity: Crosscultural Variations.* Long Grove, IL: Waveland, 1999.

———. *Neither Man Nor Woman: The Hijras of India.* Belmont, CA: Wadsworth, 1990.

Nestle, Joan, Clare Howe, and Riki Wilchins, eds. *Genderqueer: Voices from Beyond the Sexual Binary.* Boston: Alyson, 2002.

Ramet, Sandra P., ed. *Gender Reversals and Gender Cultures: Anthropological and Historical Perspectives*. New York: Routledge, 1996.

Rothblatt, Martine. *The Apartheid of Sex: A Manifesto on the Freedom of Gender*. New York: Crown, 1995.

Rudacille, Deborah. *The Riddle of Gender: Science, Activism, and Transgender Rights*. New York: Pantheon, 2005.

Serano, Julia. *Whipping Girl: A Transsexual Woman on Sexism and the Scapegoating of Femininity*. Berkeley, CA: Seal, 2007.

Sharpe, Andrew. *Transgender Jurisprudence: Dysphoric Bodies of Law*. London: Cavendish, 2002.

Straayer, Chris. *Deviant Eyes, Deviant Bodies: Sexual Re-Orientations in Film and Video*. New York: Columbia University, 1996.

Stryker, Susan, ed. *The Transgender Issue. GLQ: A Journal of Lesbian and Gay Studies*, 4:2 (1998).

Stryker, Susan, and Stephen Whittle, eds. *The Transgender Studies Reader*. New York: Routledge, 2006.

Terry, Jennifer, and Jacqueline Urla, eds. *Deviant Bodies*. Bloomington: Indiana University, 1995.

Tully, Brian. *Accounting for Transsexualism and Transhomosexuality*. London: Whiting and Birch, 1992.

Whittle, Stephen. *Respect and Equality: Transsexual and Transgender Rights*. New York: Routledge, 2002.

———. *The Transgender Debate: The Crisis Surrounding Gender Identities*. South Street, 2000.

Wilchins, Riki. *Read My Lips: Sexual Subversion and the End of Gender*. Ann Arbor: Firebrand, 1997.

BOOKS: BIOGRAPHY, AUTOBIOGRAPHY, AND FICTION

Ames, Jonathan, ed. *Sexual Metamorphosis: An Anthology of Transsexual Memoirs*. New York: Vintage, 2005.

Blumenstein, Rosalyne. *Branded T*. Bloomington, IN: First Books Library, 2003.

Boyd, Helen. *My Husband Betty: Love, Sex, and Life with a Crossdresser*. New York: Thunder's Mouth, 2003.

———. *She's Not the Man I Married: My Life with a Transgender Husband*. Berkeley, CA: Seal, 2007.

Boylan, Jennifer Finney. *She's Not There: A Life in Two Genders*. New York: Broadway, 2003.

Feinberg, Leslie. *Stone Butch Blues*. Ann Arbor, MI: Firebrand, 1993.

Green, Jamison. *Becoming a Visible Man*. Nashville, TN: Vanderbilt University, 2004.

Hodgkinson, Liz. *Michael Nee Laura: The Story of the World's First Female to Male Transsexual*. London: Columbus, 1989.

Howey, Noelle. *Dress Codes: Of Three Girlhoods—My Mother's, My Father's, and Mine*. New York: Picador, 2002.

Jorgensen, Christine. *Christine Jorgensen: A Personal Autobiography.* 2nd ed. San Francisco: Cleis, 2000.

Kailey, Matt. *Just Add Hormones: An Insider's Guide to the Transsexual Experience.* Boston: Beacon, 2005.

Khosla, Dhillon. *Both Sides Now: One Man's Journey Through Womanhood.* New York: Tarcher, 2006.

McCloskey, Deirdre N. *Crossing: A Memoir.* Chicago: University of Chicago, 1999.

Middlebrook, Diane Wood. *Suits Me: The Double Life of Billy Tipton.* Boston: Houghton Mifflin, 1998.

Nettick, Geri. *Mirrors: Portrait of a Lesbian Transsexual.* New York: Rhinoceros, 1996.

Rees, Mark Nicholas Alban. *Dear Sir or Madam: The Autobiography of a Female-to-Male Transsexual.* London: Cassell, 1996.

Roscoe, Will. *The Zuni Man-Woman.* Albuquerque: University of New Mexico, 1991.

Rose, Donna. *Wrapped in Blue: A Journey of Discovery.* Round Rock, TX: Living Legacy, 2003.

Scholinski, Daphne. *The Last Time I Wore a Dress.* New York: Riverhead, 1997.

Sullivan, Louis G. *From Female to Male: The Life of Jack B. Garland.* Boston: Alyson, 1990.

Valerio, Max Wolf. *The Testosterone Files: My Hormonal and Social Transformation from Female to Male.* Berkeley, CA: Seal, 2006.

Zander, Erica. *TransActions.* Stockholm: Periskop, 2003.

DOCUMENTARIES/FEATURE FILMS

Adventures in the Gender Trade. Directed by Kate Bornstein. New York: Filmmakers Library, 1993.

The Adventures of Priscilla, Queen of the Desert. Directed by Stephan Elliott. New York: PolyGram Video, 1994.

All About My Father (Alt Om Min Far). Directed by Eva Benestad. Norway: Oro Film, 2001.

All About My Mother (Todo sobre mi madre). Directed by Pedro Almodóvar. El Deseo S.A., 1999.

Almost Myself. Directed by Tom Murray. T. Joe Murray Videos, 2006.

The Badge. Directed by Robby Henson. Emma/Furla Films, 2002.

Beautiful Boxer. Directed by Ekachai Uekrongtham. GMM Pictures, 2003.

Boys Don't Cry. Directed by Kimberly Peirce. Beverly Hills, CA: Twentieth Century Fox Home Entertainment, 1999.

The Brandon Teena Story. Directed by Susan Muska. New York: Bless Bess Productions, 1998.

The Cockettes. Directed by Billy Weber and David Weissman. Grandelusion, 2002.

Cruel and Unusual. Directed by Janet Baus, Dan Hunt, and Reid Williams. Reid Productions, 2007. Distributed by Frameline.

The Crying Game. Directed by Neil Jordan. British Screen Productions, 1992.

Different for Girls. Directed by Richard Spence. Fox Lorber, 1997.

Female Misbehavior. Directed by Monika Treut. Germany: Hyena Films, 1992.

Flawless. Directed by Joel Schumacher. Tribeca Productions, 1999.

Gendernauts. Directed by Monika Treut. USA/Germany, 1999.

Hedwig and the Angry Inch. Directed by John Cameron Mitchell. New Line Home Entertainment, 2001.

The Iron Ladies (Satree-lex). Directed by Yongyoot Thongkongtoon. Santa Monica, CA: Strand Releasing Home Video, 2002.

Junk Box Warrior. Directed by Preeti Mistry. USA: Frameline Distribution, 2002.

Law of desire (La ley del deseo). Directed by Pedro Almodovar. New York: Cinevista Video, 1987.

M. Butterfly. Directed by David Cronenberg. Burbank, CA: Warner Home Video. 1993.

Multiple Genders: Mind and Body in Conflict. Produced by Anna Laura Malago. Princeton, NJ: Films for the Humanities and Sciences, 1998.

My Life in Pink (Ma vie en rose). Directed by Alain Berliner. Sony Pictures Classica/La Sept Cinema, 1997.

Normal. Directed by Jane Anderson. Avenue Pictures, 2003.

Orlando. Directed by Sally Potter. Adventure Pictures, 1994.

Paper Dolls (Bubot Niyar). Directed by Tomer Heymann. Strand Releasing, 2005.

Princesa. Directed by Henrique Goldman. Bac Films, 2001.

Screaming Queens: The Riot at Compton's Cafeteria. Directed by Susan Stryker and Victor Silverman. KQED/Independent Television Productions, 2005.

En Soap. Directed by Pernille Fischer Christensen. Netherlands: Garage Film AB, 2006.

Southern Comfort. Directed by Kate Davis. HBO Theatrical Documentary. New York: Q-Ball Productions, 2001.

Transamerica. Directed by Duncan Tucker. Belladonna Productions, 2005.

TransGeneration. Directed by Jeremy Simmons. Logo Entertainment, 2005.

Transsexual Menace. Directed by Rosa Von Praunheim. USA/Germany: Video Data Bank, 1996.

Venus Boyz. Directed by Gabrielle Baur. USA/Switzerland: Clock Wise Productions, 2002.

Wild Side. Directed by Sébastien Lifshitz. Maïa Films, 2004.

WEBSITES

American Civil Liberties Union: www.aclu.org

Camp Trans: http://camptrans.squarespace.com

Campus Pride: www.campuspride.net

Compton's Cafeteria Riot Commemoration: www.comptonscafeteriariot.org/main.html

FIERCE!: www.fiercenyc.org

GenderTalk.com: www.gendertalk.com

GLBT Historical Society: www.glbthistory.org

The Harry Benjamin International Gender Dysphoria Association: www.hbigda.org
International Foundation for Gender Education/Transgender Tapestry: www.ifge.org
National Center for Transgender Equality: www.nctequality.org
National Transgender Advocacy Coalition: www.ntac.org
NOVA: Sex Unknown: www.pbs.org/wgbh/nova/gender
QueerTheory.com: Transgender Schools and Support Programs:
    www.queertheory.com/academics/schools
Rachel's Web: A Transgendered Experience: http://rachels-web.com
Recommendations for Enhancing College Environments for Transsexual and Transgender
    Students: http://ai.eecs.umich.edu/people/conway/TS/College.html
The Renaissance Transgender Association: www.ren.org
Susan's Place: Transgender Resources: www.susans.org
Sylvia Rivera Law Project: www.srlp.org
Trans-Academics.org: www.trans-academics.org
TransAdvocate: www.transadvocate.com
TransBiblio: Transgender Bibliography
    www.library.uiuc.edu/circ/transgender_bibliography/transbiblio.htm
Transgender Aging Network: www.forge-forward.org/tan
Transgender American Veterans Association: www.tavausa.org
Transgender Day of Remembrance: www.dayofsilence.org
Transgendered Network International: www.tgni.com
Transgender Forum: www.tgfmall.com
The Transgender Law and Policy Institute: www.transgenderlaw.org
Transgender Law Center: www.transgenderlawcenter.org
Transgender Law Project: www.nclrights.org/projects/transgenderproject.htm
The TransHealth Education Network: www.jri.org/thed.html
TransGriot: http://transgriot.blogspot.com

SOURCES

Chapter 1

Third Wave Feminism: Stacy Gillis, Gillian Howe, and Rebecca Munford, eds., *Third Wave Feminism: A Critical Exploration* (London: Palgrave, rev. 2nd ed., 2007); Daisy Hernández and Bushra Rehman, eds., *Colonize This!: Young Women of Color on Today's Feminism* (New York: Seal, 2002).

Social Movements: Minority rights have long been a factor in U.S. politics: see Alexis de Toqueville, *Democracy in America* (New York: Penguin Classics, 2003, orig. pub. 1835, 1840); for a discussion of sexual minority movement formation, see Barry D. Adam, *The Rise of a Gay and Lesbian Movement* (Woodbridge, CT: Twayne, rev. ed., 1997).

A Biological Basis?: Joan Roughgarden, *Evolution's Rainbow: Diversity, Gender, and Sexuality in Nature and People* (Berkeley: University of California, 2004), 241–244; Deborah Rudacille, "Fear of a Pink Planet," in *The Riddle of Gender: Science, Activism, and Transgender Rights* (New York: Pantheon, 2005), 240–276. Christine Johnson revised and expanded her paper "Endocrine Disrupting Chemicals and Transsexualism," cited by Rudacille. The revised document is "Transsexualism: An Unacknowledged Endpoint of Developmental Endocrine Disruption?" MA Thesis, Environmental Studies, Evergreen State College, Olympia, WA, 2004; available online at www.antijen.org/tranadvocate /TS_EDCs.pdf.

Glossary of Terms/Gender Identity Disorder: http://en.wikipedia.org/wiki /Transgender has a well-documented article; on disorders of sexual development, which remain controversial in the intersex community, see http://dsdguidelines.org; on some of the pitfalls of cross-cultural comparisons of gender variance, see Evan Towle and Lynn Morgan, "Romancing the Transgender Native: Rethinking the Use of the 'Third Gender' Concept," in Susan Stryker and Stephen Whittle, eds., *The Transgender Studies Reader* (New York: Routledge, 2006), 666–684; the official diagnostic criteria for Gender

Identity Disorder can be found in *Diagnostic and Statistical Manual of Mental Disorders* (Washington, D.C: American Psychiatric Association, 4th ed., text revision, 2000), 535–582.

Transvestism: Magnus Hirschfeld, *The Transvestites: The Erotic Drive for Disguise*, (Buffalo, NY: Prometheus, 1991, orig. pub. 1910); **Psychopathia Transexualis:** D. O. Caldwell, "Psychopathia Transexualis," *Sexology* (vol. 16, 1949), 274-280, text available online at www.symposion.com/ijt/cauldwell/cauldwell_02.htm.

Transgender: David Valentine, *Imagining Transgender: An Ethnography of a Category* (Durham, NC: Duke University, 2007).

Subcultural Terms: Phillip Herbst, *Wimmin, Wimps and Wallflowers: An Encyclopaedic Dictionary of Gender and Sexual Orientation Bias in the United States* (Boston: Intercultural, 2001); Guy Strait, *The Lavender Lexicon: A Dictionary of Gay Words and Phrases* (San Francisco: Strait and Associates, 1964).

Why Transgender Is Such a Hot Topic Now: Susan Stryker, "(De)Subjugated Knowledges: An Introduction to Transgender Studies," in Susan Stryker and Stephen Whittle, eds., *The Transgender Studies Reader* (New York: Routledge, 2006), 1–17.

Religion and Transgender: Virginia Ramey Mollenkott, *Omnigender: A Trans-religious Approach* (Cleveland, OH: The Pilgrim Press, 2001; revised and expanded, 2007), discussion of Charles Colson, pp. 91–92; *The Transformation* (Carlos Aparicio and Susan Aikin, dirs., Frameline Distribution, 1995) offers a fascinating portrait of a male-to-female transgender person's participation in an evangelical Christian community.

Transgender and Postmodern Representation: Susan Stryker, "Christine Jorgensen's Atom Bomb: Mapping Postmodernity though the Emergence of Transsexuality," in E. Ann Kaplan and Susan Squier, eds., *Playing Dolly: Technocultural Formations, Fictions, and Fantasies of Assisted Reproduction* (New Brunswick, NJ: Rutgers University, 1999), 157–171.

Biotechnology and the Posthuman Future: Katherine Hayles, *How We Became Posthuman: Virtual Bodies in Cybernetics, Literature, and Informatics* (Chicago: University of Chicago, 1999); Judith Halberstam and Ira Livingston, eds., *Posthuman Bodies* (Bloomington: Indiana University, 1995); Marquard Smith and Joanne Morra, *The Prosthetic Impulse: From a Posthuman Present to a Biocultural Future* (Cambridge, MA: MIT, 2007).

Chapter 2

Gender-Variant History: Rudolph Dekker and Lotte C. Van der Pol, *The Tradition of Transvestitism in Early Modern Europe* (New York: St. Martin's, 1989); Leslie Feinberg, *Transgender Warriors: Making History from Joan of Arc to Dennis Rodman* (Boston: Beacon, 1996).

Regulating Public Gender: William Eskridge, *Gaylaw: Challenging the Apartheid of the Closet* (Cambridge: Harvard University, 1997); Clare Sears, "A Dress Not Belonging to His or Her Sex: Cross-Dressing Law in San Francisco, 1860–1900," PhD Dissertation, Sociology Department, University of California—Santa Cruz, 2005.

Outlawing Cross-Dressing: The quoted statute appeared in the *Revised Orders of the City and County of San Francisco* 1863; cited in William Eskridge, *Gaylaw: Challenging* *the Apartheid of the Closet* (Cambridge: Harvard University, 1997); table compiled by Clare Sears in "A Dress Not Belonging to His or Her Sex: Cross-Dressing Law in San Francisco, 1860–1900," PhD Dissertation, Sociology Department, University of California—Santa Cruz, 2005, based on data from Eskridge's *Gaylaw*.

Capitalism and Gay Identity: John D'Emilo, "Capitalism and Gay Identity," in Ann Snitow, Christine Stancell, and Sharon Thompson, eds., *Powers of Desire: The Politics of Sexuality* (New York: Monthly Review, 1983), 100–113.

Modernity and Womanhood: Joanne Meyerowitz, *Women Adrift: Women Wage Earners in Chicago, 1880–1930* (Chicago: University of Chicago Press, 1988).

First Wave Feminism: Mary Wollstonecraft, *Vindication of the Rights of Woman* (New York: Bartleby.com, 1999; Sojourner Truth, *Ain't I a Woman?* (delivered 1851, Women's Convention, Akron, Ohio), text available online at www.feminist.com/resources /artspeech/genwom/sojour.htm.

Bloomerism: Dexter C. Bloomer, *Life and Writings of Amelia Bloomer* (New York: Schocken, 1975, orig. pub. 1895).

Social Power of Medicine: Georges Canguilhem, *The Normal and Pathological,* trans. Carolyn R. Fawcett and Robert S. Cohen (New York: Zone, 1991); Michel Foucault, *The Birth of the Clinic,* trans. Sheridan Smith (New York, Vintage, 1994, orig. pub. 1963).

Early Surgical Request: Bryan Tully, *Accounting for Transsexualism and Transhomosexuality* (London: Whiting and Birch, 1992).

Ulrichs and Kertbeny: Karl Heinrich Ulrichs, *The Riddle of "Man-Manly" Love,* trans. Michael Lombardi-Nash (Buffalo: Prometheus, 1994); Hubert Kennedy, *Karl Heinrich Ulrichs: Pioneer of the Modern Gay Movement* (San Francisco: Peremptory, 2002).

Sexology: Richard von Krafft-Ebing: *Psychopathia Sexualis* (New York: Arcade, 1998, orig. pub. 1886); Jay Prosser, "Transsexuals and the Transsexologists: Inversion and the Emergence of Transsexual Subjectivity," in Lucy Bland and Laura Doan, eds., *Sexology in Culture: Labelling Bodies and Desires* (Oxford: Polity, 1998), 116–132; for information on Hirschfeld and other notable sexologists, see Erwin Haeberle's Archive for Sexology website at Humboldt University (Berlin), www2.hu-berlin.de/sexology; on Ellis, see http://en.wikipedia.org/wiki/Havelock_Ellis.

Hitler on Hirschfeld: Leslie Katz, "Life of Gay German Jewish Sexologist Honored," *Jewish News Weekly of Northern California* (June 6, 1997), text available online at www .jewishsf.com/content/2-0-/module/displaystory/story_id/6329/edition_id/118 /format/html/displaystory.html.

The Cercle Hermaphroditos: Earl Lind, *Autobiography of an Androgyne* (New York: The Medico-Legal Journal, 1918), 151; see also Earl Lind, *The Female Impersonators* (New York: The Medico-Legal Journal, 1922).

UCSF Research: Karl Bowman, *California Sex Deviates Research Act, Progress Report, 1951,* Typescript, Don Lucas Collection (San Francisco: GLBT Historical Society, 1951), 1–25; Karl Bowman, *My Years in Psychiatry, 1915–1968: An Interview with Karl M. Bowman, M.D., San Francisco, February 27 and 28, 1968* (Sacramento, CA: California Department of Mental Hygiene, 1969).

Louise Lawrence: Manuscript Journal, Louise Lawrence Collection, Kinsey Institute

(Bloomington: Indiana University); Joanne Meyerowitz, "Sex Research at the Borders of Gender: Transvestites, Transsexuals, and Alfred Kinsey," *Bulletin of the History of Medicine*, 75:1 (2001), 72–90.

Mayhem: Robert Veit Sherwin, "Legal Aspects of Male Transsexualism," in Richard Green and John Money, *Transsexualism and Sex Reassignment* (Baltimore: Johns Hopkins, 1969), 417–430.

Prince: *Virginia Prince: Pioneers of Transgendering special issue, International Journal of Transgenderism*, 8:4 (2006).

Christine Jorgensen: Christine Jorgensen, *A Personal Autobiography; 2nd ed.* (San Francisco: Cleis, 2000).

Jorgensen Correspondents: Christine Jorgensen Collection, Correspondence Files (Copenhagen: Royal Danish Library and Archives).

Popular Reception of Jorgensen: David Serlin, "Christine Jorgensen and the Cold War Closet," in *Replaceable You: Engineering the Body in Cold War America* (Chicago: University of Chicago, 2004), 159–190.

Virginia Prince Arrest: Richard Docter, *From Man to Woman: The Transgender Journey of Virginia Prince* (Los Angeles: Docter, 2004), 109–110.

Postal Crime: Charles Smith, "The Homosexual Federal Offender: A Study of 100 Cases," *The Journal of Criminal Law, Criminology, and Police Science*, 44:5 (Jan.–Feb. 1954), 582–591, quote 586.

Literature and Obscenity Cases: Jackie Hatton, "The Pornographic Empire of H. Lynn Womack: Gay Political Discourse and Popular Culture, 1955–1970," *Threshholds: Viewing Culture* 7 (Spring 1993), 9–33; Sanford Aday Collection, Special Collections (Fresno: California State University Library).

Kinsey Reports: Alfred C. Kinsey, Wardell B. Pomeroy, and Clyde E. Martin, *Sexual Behavior in the Human Male* (Philadelphia, PA: W. B. Saunders, 1948); Alfred C. Kinsey, et al., *Sexual Behavior in the Human Female*, (Philadelphia, PA: W. B. Saunders, 1953).

Early Cross-Dresser Organizations: Darrell Raynor, *A Year Among the Girls* (New York: L. Stuart, 1966); Robert Hill, *A Social History of Heterosexual Transvestism in Cold War America*, PhD Dissertation, American Studies, University of Michigan, 2007.

Drag Balls: Miss Major interview conducted by Susan Stryker, January 29, 1998, on deposit at the GLBT Historical Society, San Francisco, CA.

Chapter 3

Cooper's Donuts Incident: Lillian Faderman and Stuart Timmons, *Gay L.A.: A History of Sexual Outlaws, Power Politics, and Lipstick Lesbians* (New York: Basic, 2006), 1–2.

John Rechy: *City of Night* (New York: Grove, 1963), 96–97, 105.

Dewey's Incident: Marc Stein, *City of Sisterly and Brotherly Loves: Lesbian and Gay Philadelphia, 1945–1972* (Chicago: University of Chicago, 2000), 246–247.

Compton's Cafeteria Incident: Raymond Broshears, "History of Christopher Street West—SF," *Gay Pride: The Official Voice of the Christopher Street West Parade '72 Committee of San Francisco, California* (June 25, 1972), 8; *Screaming Queens: The Riot at Compton's Cafeteria* (Susan Stryker and Victor Silverman, dirs., Frameline Distribution, 2005);

Elizabeth Armstrong and Suzanna Crage, "Movements and Memory: The Making of the Stonewall Myth," *American Sociological Review,* 71:5 (2006), 724–751.

Tenderloin: Neil L. Shumsky and Larry M. Springer, "San Francisco's Zone of Prostitution, 1880–1934," *Journal of Historical Geography,* 7:1 (1981), 71–89; Clark Taylor, et al. *Final Report: The Tenderloin Ethnographic Research Project* (San Francisco: Hospitality House, 1977).

War-Related Prostitution Crackdowns: Allan Berube, *Coming Out Under Fire: The History of Gay Men and Women in World War II* (New York: Free Press, 2000); Xavier Maine, *The Intersexes, a History of Similisexualism as a Problem of Social Life* (New York: Arno Reprints, orig. pub. 1908), 212–226.

Midcentury Urban Transformations: Chester Hartman, *City for Sale: The Transformation of San Francisco* (Berkeley: University of California, 2002); Nan Alamilla Boyd, *Wide Open Town: A History of Queer San Francisco to 1965* (Berkeley: University of California, 2003); Gayle Rubin, "The Valley of the Kings: Leathermen in San Francisco, 1960–1990," PhD Dissertation, Anthropology, University of Michigan, 1994.

Glide Memorial United Methodist Church: Glide website, www.glide.org.

Antipoverty Campaign: Ed Hansen Papers (San Francisco: GLBT Historical Society); Don Lucas Papers (San Francisco: GLBT Historical Society).

Alinsky: Saul Alinsky, *Reveille for Radicals* (New York: Vintage, 1989, orig. pub 1946).

Homophile Activism: John D'Emilio, *Sexual Politics, Sexual Communities: The Making of a Homosexual Minority in the United States, 1940–1970* (Chicago: University of Chicago, 1983); Martin Meeker, *Contacts Desired: Gay and Lesbian Communications and Community, 1940s–1970s* (Chicago: University of Chicago, 2006).

Harry Benjamin: Harry Benjamin, *The Transsexual Phenomenon* (New York: Julian, 1966), text available online at www.symposion.com/ijt/benjamin/index.htm.

New Transgender Networks: Members of the Gay and Lesbian Historical Society, "MTF Transgender Activism in San Francisco's Tenderloin: Commentary and Interview with Elliot Blackstone," *GLQ: A Journal of Lesbian and Gay Studies,* 4:2 (1998), 349–372; Edward Sagarin, "Transvestites and Transsexuals: Boys Will Be Girls," in *Odd Man In: Societies of Deviants in America* (Chicago: Quadrangle, 1969), 111–141; "Ms. Leslie: A Transexual Counselor," *Drag,* 3:10 (1973), 34–35.

Reed Erickson: Aaron Devor and Nicholas Matte, "ONE Inc. and Reed Erickson: The Uneasy Collaboration of Gay and Trans Activism, 1964–2003," *GLQ: A Journal of Gay and Lesbian Studies,* 10:2, 179–209.

Mario Martino: Mario Martino, with Harriet, *Emergence: A Transsexual Autobiography: The First Complete Female-to-Male Story* (New York: Crown, 1977).

Stonewall: David Carter, *Stonewall: The Riots That Sparked the Gay Revolution* (St. Martin's, 2004); Martin Duberman, *Stonewall* (Penguin, 1993).

Radical Transsexual: Suzy Cooke interview conducted by Susan Stryker, January 10, 1998, on deposit at the GLBT Historical Society, San Francisco, CA.

Sylvia Rivera: "Leslie Feinberg Interviews Sylvia Rivera," text available online at www.workers.org/ww/1998/sylvia0702.php.

STAR: Stephan Cohen, *The Gay Liberation Youth Movement in New York: An Army of Lovers Cannot Fail* (New York: Routledge, 2007).

Gay Militancy: Donn Teal, *The Gay Militants* (New York: Stein and Day, 1971).

Angela K. Douglas: Angela K. Douglas, *Triple Jeopardy* (Sneeds, FL: Self-published, 1982), copy on deposit at GLBT Historical Society, San Francisco.

Chapter 4

Cockettes: Pam Tent, *Midnight at the Palace: My Life as a Fabulous Cockette* (Los Angeles: Alyson, 2004); *The Cockettes* (David Weissman and Bill Weber, dirs., Strand Releasing, 2002), **Sylvester:** Joshua Gamson, *The Fabulous Sylvester: The Legend, the Music, the Seventies in San Francisco* (New York: Picador, 2006).

NTCU Bust: Members of the Gay and Lesbian Historical Society, "MTF Transgender Activism in San Francisco's Tenderloin: Commentary and Interview with Elliot Blackstone," *GLQ: A Journal of Lesbian and Gay Studies,* 4:2 (1998), 349–372.

Sex-Change Clinics: Joanne Meyerowitz, *How Sex Changed: A History of Transsexuality in the United States* (Cambridge, MA: Harvard University, 2002), 212–226.

Trans Liberation Newsletter: Article reprinted in *Gay Sunshine,* 5 (Jan. 1971), 3.

Gay Gender Style/Clone Look: Crawford Barton, *Beautiful Men* (Los Angeles: Liberation, 1976; the Castro website, http://thecastro.net/scenes/scene05.html.

Depathologization of Homosexuality: *Changing Our Minds: The Story of Dr. Evelyn Hooker* (Richard Schmiechen, dir., Frameline Distribution, 1992); Ronald Bayer, *Homosexuality and American Psychiatry* (Princeton, NJ: Princeton University, 1987).

Feminine Mystique: Betty Friedan, *The Feminine Mystique* (New York: Norton, 2001, orig. pub. 1963).

Second Sex: Simone de Beauvoir, *The Second Sex* (New York, Vintage, 1989, orig. pub. in French, 1949).

Radical Feminism: Alice Echols, *Daring to Be Bad: Radical Feminism in America, 1967–1975* (Minneapolis: University of Minnesota, 1990).

Radicalesbians: Karla Jay, *Tales of the Lavender Menace* (New York: Basic, 1999); "The Woman-Identified Woman," in Sarah Lucia Hoagland and Julia Penelope, eds., *For Lesbians Only: A Separatist Anthology* (London: Onlywomen, 1988), 17–22.

Gay Pride 1972: James Finefrock, "A Parade by 1000 S.F. Gays," *San Francisco Examiner,* June 26, 1972; on Raymond Broshears, see "Ray Who?: A Crusader," *Gay Focus* (Jan. 15, 1982), 1–4.

Beth Elliott: Geri Nettick, as told to Beth Elliott, *Mirrors: Portrait of a Lesbian Transsexual* (New York: Masquerade, 1996).

Daughters of Bilitis History: Marcia Gallo, *Different Daughters: A History of Daughters of Bilitis and the Rise of the Lesbian Rights Movement* (Berkeley, CA: Seal, 2006).

West Coast Lesbian Feminist Conference, 1973: *The Lesbian Tide* (Apr.–May, 1973), special issue on the West Coast Lesbian Feminist Conference.

Robin Morgan at WCLFC: "Lesbianism and Feminism: Synonyms or Contradictions?" in Robin Morgan, *Going Too Far: The Personal Chronicle of a Feminist* (New York: Random House, 1977), 170–189.

Olivia/Stone Boycott: Sandy Stone (interviewed by Davina Gabrielle), "Interview with the Transsexual Vampire: Sandy Stone's Dark Gift," *TransSisters: The Journal of Transsexual Feminism*, 8 (1995), 14–33.

Mary Daly: Mary Daly, *Gyn/Ecology: The Metaethics of Radical Feminism* (Boston: Beacon, 1978).

Janice Raymond: Janice Raymond, *The Transsexual Empire: The Making of the She-Male* (Boston: Beacon, 1979, reissued with new introduction, 1994).

Raymond, Policy Implications: Janice Raymond, "Paper Prepared for the National Center for Health Care Technology on the Social and Ethical Aspects of Transsexual Surgery, June, 1980," manuscript in National Transgender Library and Archives, Special Collections (Ann Arbor: University of Michigan Library).

Second Wave Feminism: Candy Coleman, "Broken Chains: Sisters All?" *Gay Crusader* (June–July 1973), 3; Deborah Feinbloom, "Lesbian/Feminist Orientation Among Male-to-Female Transsexuals," *Journal of Homosexuality*, 2:1 (1976), 59–71; Shulamith Firestone, *The Dialectic of Sex: A Case for Feminist Revolution* (New York: Morrow, 1970), 11; C. Tami Weyant, letter to the editor, *Sister* (Aug.–Sept. 1977), 3.

Transphobic Screed: Debbie Mikuteit, letter to the editor, *Coming Up!* (San Francisco, Feb. 1986), 3–4.

GID/Standards of Care: World Professional Organization for Transgender Health (formerly Harry Benjamin International Gender Dysphoria Association), *Standards of Care* (6th rev. ed., 2001), text available online at www.wpath.org/publications_standards.cfm.

Antipornography Feminism and the State: U.S. Attorney General's Commission on Pornography: Final Report, July, 1986 (Washington, DC: United States Department of Justice, 1986), commonly referred to as the Meese Commission Report, text available online at www.porn-report.com.

Shift from Depathologizing Homosexuality to Pathologizing Gender Variance: Janice Irvine, "Boys Will Be Girls," in *Disorders of Desire: Sex and Gender in Modern American Sexology* (Philadelphia: Temple University, 1990), 229–278.

Transgender HIV: Kristen Clements-Nolle et al., "HIV Prevalence, Risk Behaviors, Health Care Use, and Mental Health Status of Transgender Persons: Implications for Public Health Intervention," *American Journal of Public Health*, 91:6 (2001), 915–921.

Lesbian/Butch/FTM Border Wars: Henry Rubin, "Border Wars: Lesbian and Transsexual Identities," in *Self-Made Men: Identity and Embodiment Among Transsexual Men* (Nashville, TN: Vanderbilt University, 2003), 77–92.

FTM Community: Joanne Meyerowitz, *How Sex Changed: A History of Transsexuality in the United States* (Cambridge, MA: Harvard University, 2002), 226–241; Jamison Green, *Becoming a Visible Man* (Nashville, TN: Vanderbilt University, 2004); Max Wolf Valerio, *The Testosterone Files: My Hormonal and Social Transformation from Female to Male* (Berkeley, CA: Seal, 2006); *What Sex Am I?* (Lee Grant, dir., HBO Films, 1985).

Lou Sullivan: Susan Stryker, "Portrait of a Transfag Drag Hag as a Young Man: The Activist Career of Louis G. Sullivan," in Kate More and Stephen Whittle, eds., *Reclaiming Gender: Transsexual Grammars at the Fin de Siècle* (London: Cassells, 1999), 62–82.

Lou Sullivan Journals and Articles: Louis Graydon Sullivan Collection, GLBT Historical Society, San Francisco, CA, on deposit at San Francisco History Center, San Francisco Public Library (Main Branch).

Chapter 5

Legislative History: Katrina C. Rose, "The Proof Is in the History: The Louisiana Constitution Recognizes Transsexual Marriages and Louisiana Sex Discrimination Law Covers Transsexuals—So Why Isn't Everyone Celebrating?" *Deakin Law Review,* 9:2 (2004), 399–460.

Transsexual Rights Committee: See www.transhistory.net/history/TH_ACLU.html.

Ari Kane and Fantasia Fair: www.cowart.com/outreach/ari.html, http://fantasiafair .org.

International Foundation for Gender Education (IFGE): See www.ifge.org.

Dallas Denny: "Five Questions with Dallas Denny," (En)Gender blog, see www .myhusbandbetty.com/?p=427.

Transgender Etymology: Robert Hill, *A Social History of Heterosexual Transvestism in Cold War America,* PhD Dissertation, American Studies, University of Michigan, 2007.

Holly Boswell: Holly Boswell, "The Transgender Alternative," *Chrysalis Quarterly,* 1:2 (Winter 1991–1992), pp. 29–31.

Feinberg: Leslie Feinberg, *Transgender Liberation: A Movement Whose Time Has Come* (New York: World View Forum, 1992); *Stone Butch Blues* (Ithica, NY: Firebrand, 1993).

Sandy Stone: Sandy Stone, "The 'Empire' Strikes Back: A Posttranssexual Manifesto," in Julia Epstein and Kristina Straub, eds., *Body Guards: The Cultural Politics of Gender Ambiguity* (New York: Routledge, 1991), 280–304.

Feminist Hybridity: Cherrie Moraga and Gloria Anzaldúa, eds., *This Bridge Called My Back: Writings by Radical Women of Color* (New York: Kitchen Table, 1983); Gloria Anzaldúa, *Borderlands/La Frontera: The New Mestiza* (San Francisco: Aunt Lute/Spinsters, 1987).

Gender/Embodiment/Technology: Donna Haraway, "A Cyborg Manifesto: Science, Technology, and Socialist Feminism in the Late Twentieth Century," in David Bell and Barbara Kennedy, eds., *The Cybercultures Reader* (New York: Routledge 1999), 291–324.

Stone/Stryker Wired Interview: Susan Stryker, "Sex and Death Among the Cyborgs," *Wired* (May 1996), 134–136.

Queer Gender and Feminism: Teresa de Lauretis, "The Technology of Gender," in *Technologies of Gender: Essays on Theory, Film, and Fiction* (Bloomington: Indiana University, 1987), 1–31.

Michel Foucault: *The History of Sexuality Volume 1: An Introduction* (New York: Vintage, 1990, orig. pub. 1978).

Barnard Conference: Carole S. Vance, *Pleasure and Danger: Exploring Female Sexuality* (Boston: Routledge and Kegan Paul, 1984).

Gayle Rubin: "Thinking Sex: Notes for a Radical Theory of the Politics of Sexuality," in Carole Vance, ed., *Pleasure and Danger* (Boston: Routledge and Kegan Paul, 1984).

Judith Butler: *Gender Trouble: Feminism and the Subversion of Identity* (New York: Routledge, 1990); *Bodies That Matter: On the Discursive Limits of "Sex"* (New York and London: Routledge, 1993).

AIDS Activism and Trans Community: *International Journal of Transgenderism* special issue *Transgender and HIV: Assessment, Risk, Care,* 3:1-2 (Jan.–June 1999); Juana Rodriquez, *Queer Latinidad: Identity Practices, Discursive Spaces* (New York: New York University, 2003).

AIDS and Queer: David Halperin, *Saint=Foucault* (Oxford, UK: Oxford University, 1997).

Transgender Nation: Anne Ogborn interview by Susan Stryker (July 5, 1998), audiotape in author's possession; Susan Stryker, "Transgender History, Homonormativity, and Disciplinarity," *Radical History Review,* 100 (2007), 144–157.

March on Washington: Phyllis Randolph Frye, "Facing Discrimination, Organizing for Freedom: The Transgender Community," in John D'Emilio, William Turner, and Urvashi Vaid, eds., *Creating Change: Sexuality, Public Policy, and Civil Rights* (New York: St. Martin's, 2000), 451–468.

ISNA: Cheryl Chase, "Hermaphrodites with Attitude: Mapping the Emergence of Intersex Political Activism," *GLQ: Journal of Gay and Lesbian Studies,* 4:2 (1998), 189–211.

Intersex "Dangerous" to Society: Suzanne Kessler, *Lessons from the Intersexed* (New Brunswick, NJ: Rutgers University, 1998).

Michigan Womyn's Music Festival: See www.michfest.com; Emi Koyama, "Whose Feminism Is It Anyway: The Unspoken Racism of the Trans Inclusion Debate," in Susan Stryker and Stephen Whittle, eds., *The Transgender Studies Reader* (New York: Routledge, 2006), 698–705; "Roundtable: A Fest in Distress," Michigan/Trans Controversy Archive: http://eminism.org/michigan/documents.html.

Southern Comfort: Conference, see www.sccatl.org; film, *Southern Comfort* (Kate Davis, dir., Q-Ball Productions, 2002).

International Conference on Transgender Law and Employment Policy (ICTLEP): See www.transgenderlegal.com/ictlephis1.htm.

Transgender and Race: Martine Rothblatt, *The Apartheid of Sex: A Manifesto on the Freedom of Gender* (New York: Crown, 1995).

Riki Anne Wilchins/Transexual Menace/GenderPAC: Riki Anne Wilchins, *Read My Lips: Sexual Subversion and the End of Gender* (Ithaca, NY: Firebrand, 1997); *Transsexual Menace* (Rosa Von Praunheim, dir., Praunheim Filmproduktion, 1996); see www.gpac.org.

San Francisco Human Rights Commission Report: Jamison Green, *Investigation into Discrimination Against Transgendered People: A Report of the San Francisco Human Rights Commission* (San Francisco: Human Rights Commission, 1994).

Remembering Our Dead: See www.gender.org/remember/index.html.

Trans Academics: Robin Wilson, "Transgender Scholars Defy Tradition, Seek to Be Heard," *Chronicle of Higher Education* (orig. pub. Feb. 6, 1998), pp. A10+; see online at http://chronicle.com/colloquy/98/transgender/background.htm.

Body Alchemy: Loren Cameron, *Body Alchemy: Transsexual Portraits* (San Francisco: Cleis, 1996); see www.lorencameron.com.

Mariette Pathy Allen: *Transformations: Crossdressers and Those Who Love Them* (New York: Dutton, 1989); *The Gender Frontier* (Heidelberg, Germany: Kehrer Verlag, 2003).

Mid-1990s Media Coverage: Richard Levine, "Crossing the Line: Are Transsexuals at the Forefront of a Revolution, or Just Reinforcing Old Stereotypes About Men and Women?" *Mother Jones* 19:3 (May–June 1994), pp. 43+; Amy Bloom, "The Body Lies," *New Yorker* (July 18, 1994), pp. 38+; Carey Goldberg, "Shunning 'He' and 'She,' They Fight for Respect," *New York Times*, (Sept. 8, 1996).

Zines: Queer Zine Archive Project, see www.qzap.org/v4; see also CatalogQ.net to search many other zines by name.

Jamison Green: Jamison Green, *Becoming a Visible Man* (Nashville, TN: Vanderbilt University, 2004), see www.jamisongreen.com.

Max Wolf Valerio: Max Wolf Valerio, *The Testosterone Files: My Hormonal and Social Transformation from Female to Male* (Berkeley, CA: Seal, 2006), see www.maxwolfvalerio.com.

Jennifer Boylan: Jennifer Finney Boylan, *She's Not There: A Life in Two Genders* (New York: Broadway, 2003).

Helen Boyd: Helen Boyd, *My Husband Betty: Love, Sex, and Life with a Crossdresser* (New York: Thunder's Mouth, 2003), *She's Not the Man I Married: My Life with a Transgender Husband* (Berkeley, CA: Seal, 2007), see www.myhusbandbetty.com.

Nobody Passes: Matt Bernstein Sycamore, aka Mattilda, *Nobody Passes: Rejecting the Rules of Gender and Conformity* (Berkeley, CA: Seal, 2007).

Transgender Legal Activism in the 1990s: Excellent resources at www.transgenderlaw.org.

Transgender Rights: Paisley Currah and Shannon Minter, *Transgender Equality: A Handbook for Activists and Policymakers* (Washington, DC: National Gay and Lesbian Task Force, 2000), 17, see http://thetaskforce.org/downloads/reports/reports/TransgenderEquality.pdf.

Employment Non-Discrimination Act (ENDA): See www.unitedENDA.org.

INDEX

A

abortion: 98; see also reproductive rights
academic study: Erickson's patronage of
80; formalization of GID 111–112;
recent 124; on transgender biology
93–94; transgender studies program
131–132, 144
acceptance, of difference: 5–6
"A Dress Not Belonging to His or
Her Sex: Cross-Dressing Law in San
Francisco, 1860–1900" (Sears): 33
AIDS: 113–114, 132–134
Allen, Mariette Pathy: 145
anatomy, reproductive: 8–9
androgynes: 41
androgynous style: 100
anti-Communism: 51–52
antipathic sexual instinct: 38
antipornography campaigns: 112
antitransgender discourses: 106–111
Anzaldúa, Gloria: 124–125
Araujo, Gwen: 143
asexuality: 16
assumptions: gendered 7; socially
constructed 25–26
attire: 35, 91, 95
Autobiography of an Androgyne (Lind):
41
autosexuality: 16

B

Baby Boom generation: 53
backlash, 1970s cultural: 92
Belt, Elmer: 45
Benjamin, Dr. Harry: as colleague of
Hirschfield 40; Erickson's patronage
of 80; on gender identity 73; GID as
legacy of 111; "mayhem" case 44, 45;
promotion of "transsexual" 18, 49
Bible, the: 27
biology: as root of transgender urge 6,
9; and transgender "pathology" 37;
university research on 93–94
bisexuality: 16, 84
Blackstone, Elliott: 75, 76, 81, 92
Bloomer, Amelia: 35
bodies: boundaries, as subjective 127;
intersex 139; as regulated by the state
51; sex as culturally placed on 132;
"technocultural" 125
Bodies That Matter: On the Discursive
Limits of "Sex" (Butler): 131–132
Body Alchemy (Cameron): 144
body language: 12
body shape: 9–10
book burning, Nazi: 40
Bornstein, Kate: 144
Bowie, David: 91
Bowman, Karl: 41–44
Brandon, Teena: 142

T

ACKNOWLEDGMENTS

Thanks to Brooke Warner at Seal Press for asking me to write this book in the first place; to Denise Silva for guiding it through the initial stages and for compiling the Further Reading and Resources; and to Jennie Goode for (her) grace under (my) pressure in seeing the manuscript across the finish line. Thanks as well to my research assistant in Vancouver, Sarah Sparks, and to Denali Dalton Toevs for giving up part of our Thanksgiving vacation together to help me wrap up a few final details. I'd also like to thank two colleagues, Joanne Mayerowitz and C. Jacob Hale, for many years of conversation and shared research collaboration on transgender history. As always, my deepest love and appreciation to Kim Klausner for making her life with me.

ABOUT THE AUTHOR

© Kim Klausner

SUSAN STRYKER earned her PhD in U.S. history at the University of California— Berkeley in 1992 and later held a postdoctoral fellowship in sexuality studies at Stanford University. She was executive director of the GLBT Historical Society in San Francisco from 1999 until 2003. In addition to numerous scholarly articles and magazine pieces, she is coauthor of *Gay by the Bay: A History of Queer Culture in the San Francisco Bay Area* (1996); contributing editor of the transgender studies special issue of *GLQ: A Journal of Lesbian and Gay Studies* (1998); author of *Queer Pulp: Perverse Passions in the Golden Age of the Paperback* (2001); codirector of the Emmy Award–winning public television documentary *Screaming Queens: The Riot at Compton's Cafeteria* (2005); and coeditor of the Lambda Literary Award–winning *Transgender Studies Reader*. She held the Ruth Wynn Woodward Endowed Chair in women's studies at Simon Fraser University in Vancouver, 2007–08, and currently teaches gender studies at Harvard University.

CREDITS

Chapter 1

Excerpt from *Evolution's Rainbow* by Joan Roughgarden is reprinted with permission of University of California Press. © 2004.

Casa Susanna image courtesy of Michel Hurst and Robert Swope, from Casa Susanna. © Power House Books.

Diagnostic criteria for gender disorders is reprinted with permission from the *Diagnostic and Statistical Manual of Mental Disorders, Fourth Edition, Text Revision*, © 2000. American Psychiatric Association.

"Something Like a Brother" cartoon image is reprinted with permission from CartoonStock. © www.CartoonStock.com.

Chapter 2

"Municipal Laws Prohibiting Wearing Dress of Opposite Sex" chart compiled by Clare Sears in "A Dress Not Belonging to His or Her Sex: Cross-Dressing Law in San Francisco, 1860–1900," PhD dissertation, Sociology Department, University of California—Santa Cruz, 2005, based on data from William Eskridge, *Gaylaw: Challenging the Apartheid of the Closet* (Cambridge: Harvard University Press, 1997).

Velazquez/Buford image appears in *The Woman in Battle: The Civil War Narrative of Loreta Janeta Velazquez, Cuban Woman and Confederate Soldier*, © University of Wisconsin Press.

Book burning in Berlin, Germany, 1933, was part of the exhibition "Nazi Book Burnings and the American Response" by Steve Goodell and is reprinted with permission of the United States Holocaust Memorial Museum, courtesy of National Archives and Records Administration, College Park. *The views or opinions expressed in this book and the context in which the images are used do not necessarily reflect the views or policy of, nor imply approval or endorsement by, the United States Holocaust Memorial Museum.*

Excerpt from *The Transvestites: The Erotic Drive to Cross-Dress,* by Magnus Hirschfeld, translated by Michael A. Lombardi-Nash (Amherst, NY: Prometheus Books, 1991). © 1991 by Michael A. Lombardi-Nash. All rights reserved. Reprinted with permission of the publisher.

Louise Lawrence image © Vern Bullough Collection, Oviatt Library, Cal State Northridge.

Christine Jorgensen image © The Royal Library, Copenhagen.

Excerpt from Drag Balls: Miss Major is taken from an interview conducted by Susan Stryker, January 29, 1998, on deposit at the GLBT Historical Society, San Francisco

African American drag queens image is reprinted by permission of the GLBT Historical Society of Northern California. © Henri Leleu Collection 1997.

Chapter 3

Excerpt from *City of Night,* by John Rechy (New York: Grove, 1963) © 1963. All rights reserved. Reprinted with permission of the publisher.

Gene Compton's Cafeteria frame grab is provided courtesy of Susan Stryker and was captured from the documentary *Screaming Queens: The Riot at Compton's Cafeteria,* directed by Susan Stryker and Victor Silverman.

Marsha P. Johnson image is provided courtesy of Amy Coleman. © Amy Coleman.

Reed Erickson image is from the collection of Aaron Devor. © Aaron Devor.

"Tenderloin Transexual" page spread is from *Vanguard* magazine, a zine published from the late '60s to early '70s. Image provided by the GLBT Historical Society of Northern California.

Excerpt from Radical Transsexual: Suzy Cooke is taken from an interview conducted by Susan Stryker, January 10, 1998, on deposit at the GLBT Historical Society, San Francisco.

Vanguard magazine cover, Volume 1, Number 1, was provided by the GLBT Historical Society of Northern California.

Chapter 4

"Illustration of Male-to-Female Surgical Technique, 1958," is taken from *Homosexuality, Transvesticism, and Change of Sex* (Springfield, IL: Charles Thomas, 1958), 64. All rights reserved. Reprinted with permission of the publisher.

Excerpt from *Trans Liberation Newsletter* was reprinted in *Gay Sunshine*, 5 (Jan. 1971).

Beth Elliot image is provided courtesy of Richard McCaffrey. © Richard McCaffrey.

Excerpt from Robin Morgan at WCLFC: "Lesbianism and Feminism: Synonyms or Contradictions?" in Robin Morgan, *Going Too Far: The Personal Chronicle of a Feminist*. © Random House. 1977. All rights reserved. Reprinted with permission of the publisher.

Excerpt from Shulamith Firestone, *The Dialectic of Sex: A Case for Feminist Revolution* (New York: Morrow, 1970). Copyright © 2003, Farrar, Straus, and Giroux.

Excerpt from "Transphobic Screed: Debbie Mikuteit," letter to the editor, was taken from *Coming Up!* (San Francisco, Feb. 1986), and provided by the GLBT Historical Society of Northern California.

Lou Sullivan journal entries are reprinted by permission of the GLBT Historical Society of Northern California. From the Lou Sullivan Collection.

Lou Sullivan image is provided courtesy of Mariette Pathy Allen. © Mariette Pathy Allen.

Chapter 5

Excerpts from Stone/Stryker *Wired* Interview: Susan Stryker, "Sex and Death Among the Cyborgs," compiled for *Wired* magazine (May 1996).

Transgender HIV poster was provided by the GLBT Historical Society of Northern California.

Body Alchemy poster was provided by the GLBT Historical Society of Northern California. Photo for the poster by Loren Rex Cameron © Loren Rex Cameron.

Antony Hegarty of the ensemble Antony and the Johnsons. Photo © Pieter M. van Hattem, February 28, 2005.

"Human Rights Laws in the United States That Explicitly Include Transgendered People" chart reprinted from Paisley Currah and Shannon Minter, *Transgender Equality: A Handbook for Activists and Policymakers* (Washington, DC: National Gay and Lesbian Task Force, 2000).

SELECTED TITLES FROM SEAL PRESS

For more than thirty years, Seal Press has published groundbreaking books. By women. For women. Visit our website at www.sealpress.com, and our blog at www. sealpress.com/blog.

A History of U.S. Feminisms by Rory Dicker. $12.95, 1-58005-234-7. A concise introduction to feminism from the late 19th century through today.

Whipping Girl: A Transsexual Woman on Sexism and the Scapegoating of Femininity by Julia Serano. $15.95, 1-58005-154-5. Biologist and trans woman Julie Serrano reveals a unique perspective on femininity, masculinity, and gender identity.

The Testosterone Files: My Hormonal and Social Transformation from Female to Male by Max Wolf Valerio. $15.95, 1-58005-173-1. A gripping transsexual memoir that focuses on testosterone's role in the author's emotional, perceptual, and physical transformation.

Nobody Passes: Rejecting the Rules of Gender and Conformity edited by Mattilda a.k.a Matt Bernstein Sycamore. $15.95, 1-58005-184-7. A timely and thought-provoking collection of essays confronts and challenges the notion of belonging by examining the perilous intersections of identity, categorization, and community.

She's Not the Man I Married: My Life with a Transgender Husband by Helen Boyd. $15.95, 1-58005-193-6. Taking up where *My Husband Betty* left off, this moving account of a wife's examination of her relationship with her cross-dressing partner proves to be the ultimate love story.